Doing Business with Beauty

Perspectives on a Multiracial America
Joe R. Feagin, Texas A&M University, series editor

The racial composition of the United States is rapidly changing. Books in the series will explore various aspects of the coming multiracial society, one in which European-Americans are no longer the majority and where issues of white-on-black racism have been joined by many other challenges to white dominance.

Titles:

Melanie Bush, *Breaking the Code of Good Intentions*

Amir Mavasti and Karyn McKinney, *Unwelcome Immigrants: Middle Eastern Lives in America*

Richard Rees, *Shades of Difference: A History of Ethnicity in America*

Katheryn Russell-Brown, *Protecting Our Own: Race, Crime, and African Americans*

Adia Harvey Wingfield, *Doing Business with Beauty: Black Women, Hair Salons, and the Racial Enclave Economy*

Forthcoming titles include:

Erica Chito Childs, *Fade to Black and White*

Elizabeth M. Aranda, *Emotional Bridges to Puerto Rico: Migration, Return Migration, and the Struggles of Incorporation*

Doing Business with Beauty

Black Women, Hair Salons,
and the Racial Enclave Economy

Adia Harvey Wingfield

ROWMAN & LITTLEFIELD PUBLISHERS, INC.
Lanham • Boulder • New York • Toronto • Plymouth, UK

ROWMAN & LITTLEFIELD PUBLISHERS, INC.

Published in the United States of America
by Rowman & Littlefield Publishers, Inc.
A wholly owned subsidary of The Rowman & Littlefield Publishing Group, Inc.
4501 Forbes Boulevard, Suite 200, Lanham, Maryland 20706
www.rowmanlittlefield.com

Estover Road
Plymouth PL6 7PY
United Kingdom

British Library Cataloguing in Publication Information Available

Library of Congress Cataloging-in-Publication Data:

Wingfield, Adia Harvey, 1977–
  Doing business with beauty : black women, hair salons, and the racial enclave
economy / Adia Harvey Wingfield.
       p. cm. — (Perspectives on multicultural America series)
  Includes bibliographical references.
  ISBN-13: 978-0-7425-6116-8 (cloth : alk. paper)
  ISBN-10: 0-7425-6116-X (cloth : alk. paper)
  1. Minority business enterprises—United States. 2. Women-owned business
enterprises—United States. 3. Businesswomen—United States. 4. Beauty shops—
United States. 5. Beauty operators—United States. I. Title.
  HD2358.5.U6S65 2008
  338.6'4220973—dc22   2007042298

Printed in the United States of America

⊗™ The paper used in this publication meets the minimum requirements of
American National Standard for Information Sciences—Permanence of Paper
for Printed Library Materials, ANSI/NISO Z39.48-1992.

This book is dedicated to my family:
Mom, Dad, Amina, and especially John

Contents

Foreword
Joe R. Feagin
Texas A&M University

In the first book by a secular American intellectual, *Notes on the State of Virginia* (1785), Thomas Jefferson accented what he viewed as the superior physical features of white Americans and the inferior physical features of black Americans. For Jefferson, the skin color of white Americans was naturally superior: "Are not the fine mixtures of red and white, the expressions of every passion by greater or less suffusions of colour in the one, preferable to that eternal monotony, which reigns in the countenances, that immoveable veil of black which covers all the emotions of the other race?"[1] Beauty and whiteness were thus closely associated in his mind. In this passage, Jefferson added that the "superior beauty" of whites was demonstrated in their "flowing hair" and "more elegant symmetry" of form. Such racist images were linked to Jefferson's then-new concept of a hierarchy of human "races." A leading western intellectual of his era, Jefferson played a central role in the early development of a white racial frame, a broad racist framing of black Americans as an inferior "race" that has persisted in most white minds to the present day.

Created and maintained by whites now for centuries, this white racial frame involves an organized set of racist stereotypes, images, and emotions, as well as of inclinations to discriminate, that are consciously or unconsciously expressed in the routine operation of this society's major institutions.[2] In the case of most white Americans, the racial frame has included negative stereotypes, images, emotions, and discriminatory inclinations in regard to African Americans and other Americans of color, as well as positive views of whites and white institutions. For most of the first 350 years of

North American colonization and development, this racist frame strongly rationalized and buttressed slavery and legal segregation, and since the end of legal segregation in the late 1960s, it has continued to rationalize and buttress contemporary incarnations of antiblack racism and other types of discrimination.

This strong racial frame captures territory in the mind and makes it difficult to get whites (and others) to think about this society in terms other than those of the accepted racial frame. Particular stereotypes in this racist frame, such as those still targeting black bodies, resist evidence that counters them because of how deeply these views have been implanted in white minds. As a result, most whites do not approach new encounters with black Americans with minds that are blank slates open freely to new information and interpretations, but rather with minds framed in terms of traditional white-racist thinking, interpretations, and inclinations.

Today, black Americans, including black girls and women, still face much racist imaging and commentary in the media and advertising that suggests that black bodies are not as beautiful as other bodies. Indeed, in the last several years, numerous prominent media personalities have made it clear that black hairstyles and other body imagery are part of their white racist framing of black women. One 2007 incident involved the prominent radio talk-show host, Don Imus, who commented that the Rutgers University women's basketball team was a group of "nappy-headed hos." Natural black hairstyles are thus viewed by many whites as ugly, undesirable, or extreme. Even major U.S. companies and agencies, such as Six Flags of America and Marriott Hotels, have banned or set restrictions on black hairstyles like cornrows and dreadlocks. The Six Flags firm called the latter "extreme hairstyles." The Baltimore Police Department banned hairstyles worn primarily by black employees, but backed down after protests. Such a national atmosphere creates intensely negative experiences for black girls and women with regard to their bodies.

In one interview study that I conducted, a black female honors student at a historically white university explained that her parents had "tried to instill in me that I was a beautiful person, that my blackness was a beautiful thing, that the fact that I braided my hair was fine, that I didn't have a perm was fine. But when you're like, nine, ten, eleven, you tend not to listen to your parents, and you tend to listen to everything else, which is white people . . . with *Teen* magazine and *Seventeen* magazine flung in my face all the time, Barbie dolls flung in my face all the time, soap operas with all these white folks with blonde hair and blue eyes."

Showing significant resistance to conventional white beauty models, this student's parents taught her well the lesson that her skin and hair were beautiful. Given four centuries of experience with systemic racism, African Americans have developed a strong resistance culture and counter framing that often enables them to better resist the dominant racial frame. Most African Americans share a counterframe that includes collective memories of oppression and resistance strategies to that oppression, passed down over generations.

A central purpose of this fine ethnographic study of nearly two dozen black beauty salon owners by sociologist Adia Harvey Wingfield is to critique the mainstream entrepreneurship literatures for ignoring the past and present development and importance of black businesses. Adding substantially to this literature, Harvey Wingfield demonstrates that African Americans have a long and significant history of entrepreneurship, entrepreneurship usually conducted under racially oppressive conditions. Thus, in the first decade of U.S. apartheid, of early 1900s legal segregation, the black hair care industry was developed substantially by black female entrepreneurs, by pioneers like Madame C. J. Walker. Countering the racist framing of their day, these entrepreneurs accented in their marketing and other business presentations the beauty and attractiveness of black women. Today, black beauty salons are a large sector of American business, a multibillion-dollar industry, and in recent years there has been a significant national growth in black female entrepreneurs in this and other business arenas.

Reviewing the historical development and contemporary growth of black businesses, including beauty salons, Harvey Wingfield offers an original conceptual analysis of the *racial enclave economy*. The relevant social science literature focuses on *ethnic entrepreneurship*—the *middleman minorities* and *ethnic enclaves*—thereby generally ignoring the impact of the systemic racism that targeted African Americans seeking to develop businesses. Traditional ethnic entrepreneurship research shows that nonblack immigrants frequently do better in business than black Americans, yet largely fails to incorporate into this entrepreneurial theorizing the reality that black businesses have historically been excluded or restricted by whites from serving populations other than black Americans.

All of the black female entrepreneurs interviewed by Harvey Wingfield come from working-class backgrounds and their successful beauty salons have enabled them to move up economically. Harvey Wingfield offers rare insights into the everyday lives of black working class women today, lives that social scientists have for too long mostly ignored. These salon operators have succeeded in a world where racial discrimination excludes them from many good jobs and business opportunities. From Harvey Wingfield's poignant interviews, we see the substantial employment discrimination that these black women have faced in the low-wage job markets typically available to working-class black women. The stereotypes of the traditional racial frame are firmly implanted in employers' heads, and black working-class women seeking employment are often seen as lazy, unreliable, touchy, or otherwise problematical. This institutionalized discrimination not only limits their movement up in the white-dominated economic sectors but also is a major generator of the racial enclave business economy—one that, ironically, has provided significant opportunities for African American women who develop businesses to serve other African Americans.

However, the road to economic success has not been easy for these beauty salon owners, because of numerous discriminatory barriers in the business world. Harvey Wingfield's entrepreneurs report much difficulty in getting financial support for their business development efforts. Not one of their businesses has been financed by banks, from which they have had trouble getting any loans; rather, their efforts have been financed by friends and family members or by their own savings from low-wage employment.

Much of Harvey Wingfield's probing and original analysis is about racialized space. Much of the social, economic, and political space traversed by Americans of all backgrounds was originally created, and is still substantially controlled, by white Americans. The job and business worlds are still principally white spaces in terms of normative structures, their better-paid workers' characteristics, the middle and upper reaches of their power-status hierarchies, and their racial pathologies. As African Americans move from their homes into public places such as streets, malls, and other white-owned businesses, they have the least protection against the full range of overt antiblack behavior by whites. A black person venturing into historically white spaces will often learn from the attitudes, stares, and other actions of whites that such sites are still "for whites only," or at least that whites determine who can be present and comfortable.

The black female entrepreneurs interviewed by Harvey Wingfield are aware of the problem of white-controlled space and have intentionally created a *nurturing and welcoming* environment for the black women who come to their salons. These entrepreneurs report going into the hair industry in order to make black women feel beautiful and comfortable. They create a countering social space, one in which black female beauty is honored and celebrated. Black women have here created important social spaces where they can be in control of what is said and what is done. The typical black beauty shop's atmosphere and structure challenges numerous aspects of the systemic gendered racism that black women face, such as by providing a safe space for them to discuss an array of personal, social, and political topics. In these salons, we observe black women actively using a counterframe to question and resist various racist ideas and ideologies, both those that are overt and those that are subtle. The beauty salon offers some black-controlled space for developing resistance to the dominant racist frame and the racist institutions it reinforces.

Harvey Wingfield describes well the *helping ideology* that has developed in most of the black beauty salons in regard to stylists and clients. The shops provide very supportive places for younger black women to begin work. The everyday work of these black female stylists is greatly valued and praised here, in sharp contrast to the way that the work of black women is often devalued in many other workplaces. Once valued by their female employers, moreover, their work is usually valued by their families and communities.

Because of the white racial frame's negative images of black women and their bodies, white beauty salon owners have often been reluctant or unwilling to serve black women and their hair needs. (Black women's hair also tends to require more work than that of white women.) Black beauty salons are places where black hair can be straightened to fit a white hair image; however, ever since the 1960s "black is beautiful" and Civil Rights movements, many black salons have expanded hairstyling services to include an array of more natural hair styles that do not involve straightening. Natural hair styles with African and Afro-Caribbean origins—such as braided cornrows, other braiding, afros, and dreadlocks—have become much more popular. Adopting these natural styles is seen by many black Americans, women and men, as rejecting white-oriented images of beauty and embracing with pride their own natural beauty and aesthetic. Black beauty salons are thus, in part, centers of black female resistance to white-racist beauty norms.

Harvey Wingfield does show that the beauty salons do not escape the impact of systemic gendered racism even as they create safe spaces for women. She suggests that, although hair straightening is chosen by some black women only to make curly hair more controllable, other black women still get hair straightening services because of conformity to aspects of the white hair image. Harvey Wingfield also cites examples of conversations among several black owners and clients in which they occasionally describe the behavior of certain black people in language influenced by antiblack stereotypes from the white racist frame, thereby revealing some black internalization of that damaging racist frame.

In this consistently savvy and honest analysis, Harvey Wingfield not only provides an excellent and very detailed ethnography about the often forgotten lives of black working-class women but also expands substantially the concept of systemic racism that my students and I have previously developed.

She does this by showing where and how the operation of systemic racism in the United States is constantly gendered. The systemic racism framework encourages a researcher to examine the structural depths and historical contexts of the empirical reality being studied, and this Harvey Wingfield does well in her analysis of black beauty salons. She develops an original analysis of how they operate in everyday racialized worlds and how they often succeed in their own black-female-created and controlled spaces. Harvey Wingfield thus moves our theoretical understandings substantially in the direction of assessing "systemic gendered racism," her term for a concept that should be useful in much further research. In her perspective and data, systemic racism is routinely gendered and thereby deeply embedded in many aspects of this society, yet at the same time regularly countered and resisted by ever-courageous black Americans like the women so well portrayed here in their own black-controlled spaces.

Acknowledgments

This book owes an enormous debt to the women who participated in this project. I am greatly appreciative of the respondents for agreeing to devote their time and energy toward being interviewed for this study.

This project was supported by many senior colleagues whose feedback and insight helped me to clarify my ideas and present them more soundly and persuasively. Katrina Bell McDonald, Andrew Cherlin, and Beverly Silver read early versions of this work and provided valuable feedback. Additionally, Charles Gallagher, Joya Misra, and Mindy Stombler offered exceptionally helpful suggestions on various portions of this manuscript. Most of all, I am especially indebted to Joe Feagin for championing this project and extending his wise and insightful editorial guidance. At Rowman & Littlefield Publishers, I am grateful to Michael McGandy and Alan McClare for their support of this project. Gail Markle and Ayana Cofer also provided invaluable research assistance. Gail's attention to detail, efficiency, and work ethic were especially crucial in enabling me to complete this project in a timely fashion. Finally, this work was partially supported by a Research Initiation Grant from Georgia State University.

On a personal level, the support and encouragement I received from friends and family was instrumental. My parents, William and Brenda Harvey, cheered me on when I felt like quitting; my sister, Amina Harvey, provided constant reassurance whenever I got tired or grumpy. Pam Nichols and Geneene Baxter were supportive as always, and I must acknowledge that Bernadine Harvey-Walker had the foresight to predict that I would write this book several years before I actually did so. I would also like to thank Ashley Brown, Karmen Davis, Kamola Gray, Felicia Jackson, and Dee Stiff Roberts for their friendship and support over the years. Tracy Leaman, Rebecca Romo, and Katherine Opello are also wonderful women whose friendship I value and treasure. I also owe thanks to Brandon Wingfield for trying to fix the computer when I freaked out over malfunctioning footnotes, and for being patient when I had to work instead of having fun. Last but not least, I thank John Harvey Wingfield who, during the entire process, has remained my best friend and my biggest champion.

Introduction

I first met Tanisha[1] when I was conducting research on black women entrepreneurs. I was interested in studying whether entrepreneurship in the hair industry allowed black women to experience socioeconomic advancement. A respondent referred me to 25-year-old Tanisha, informing me that her experience with salon ownership was an important story worth hearing. I met with Tanisha at her salon, a cozy, well-lit shop located off of a busy city street. As we talked, Tanisha shared that salon ownership had been a great investment for her. She hadn't done particularly well in high school and had no plans to attend college. She also was a single parent to a 6-year-old son. Owning a salon, she told me, offered her the flexibility and financial security to care for him and to provide for his needs. She casually mentioned that the six-figure income she earned as a salon owner had enabled her to buy a home in a middle-class suburb, a new car, and would provide the necessary economic capital to open another salon in a different part of the country.

After leaving the interview, I reflected on the similarities and differences between Tanisha and myself. We were both black women and both 25, but my experiences varied from Tanisha's in that I grew up solidly middle class, had completed college, and was employed in a professional occupation. Yet despite the advantages of my middle-class upbringing, Tanisha's financial success definitely stood in stark contrast to the underpaid but overworked life of a college professor. It was certainly enough to throw into sharp relief my career path in academia, where it would be a long time before my annual income matched Tanisha's, and enough for me to consider whether I had any potentially lucrative talents that were going unused while I spent hours in my campus office glued to my computer screen endlessly revising and re-submitting papers.

As I continued to interview black women salon owners, I found that while Tanisha was the most economically successful of all the women with whom I spoke, many aspects of her story were actually not that unique. For a number of working-class black women, entrepreneurship in the hair industry offered notable economic and social rewards. Often, these women were able to use entrepreneurship as a way to establish economic security that was unavailable through other means. Salon ownership in particular became a strategy for improving—or creating—the financial stability that was often elusive in other contexts. In metropolitan areas, black women can easily command six-figure salaries as beauty salon owners.[2] Those in nonmetropolitan areas often earn salaries that are commensurate with white-collar professionals. As one of my respondents stated, the hair industry was really "a field where black women could do well."

Despite black women's rapid growth among the ranks of entrepreneurs, their entrepreneurial experiences are not usually the ones that generate the most attention in either academic or mainstream sources. While the number of businesses owned by black women has increased by 147 percent between 1997 and 2006, knowledge of black women entrepreneurs' experiences, challenges, and motivations is actually quite limited.[3] The black women business owners who have recently been the subject of news articles and media stories are often well educated black women who, frustrated by glass ceilings of corporate America, turned to entrepreneurship as an alternative option.[4] These women's experiences point to a pattern of black professional women who consider entrepreneurship as a means by which they can work independently of the pressures imposed by corporate cultures that are not necessarily welcoming or hospitable to black women.

Black women like Tanisha and the other respondents who are represented in this book are not part of this cadre of black professional women who seek entrepreneurship to escape the racism and sexism in corporate work. In contrast to black professional women, the women interviewed for this book lack the class privilege that often accompanies white-collar employment in corporate America. Like their black professional counterparts, these women experience racism and sexism; unlike them, the racism and sexism these women encounter is further complicated by class inequality. Their experiences and their lives are shaped by the intersections of race, gender, and class. These intersections construct their work as entrepreneurs in a way that diverges from the entrepreneurial patterns that are normally given attention in media outlets and in sociological research.

This book is my attempt to fill this void by focusing on black working-class women's experiences with entrepreneurship. I argue that the scant attention paid to black working-class women's entrepreneurial activity represents an omission in the existing research, rather than any shortage of entrepreneurial activity on the part of these women. Further, I suggest that existing theoretical frameworks used to study entrepreneurship fail to capture the complexities and specifics of these women's experiences. To this end, I develop the theoretical concept of the racial enclave economy as a more precise framework for assessing black women's entrepreneurial ventures. Within the contours of this theoretical frame, I suggest that intersections of race and gender are paramount for understanding black working-class women's entrepreneurial ventures.

Chapter 1 of this book establishes the difference between race and ethnicity and details the theoretical concept of systemic racism. I then extend this framework by considering the gendered nature of systemic racism, and contend that systemic gendered racism shapes black women's experiences in social, economic, political, and other spheres. I also summarize the relevant literature on ethnic entrepreneurship, paying particular attention to the primary theoretical frames—middleman minority and ethnic enclave entrepreneurship—through which ethnic entrepreneurship is generally understood. I argue that gendered racism is systemic and explains the entrepreneurial experiences of racial minorities more precisely than the existing ethnic entrepreneurship paradigms. I also document how the systemic nature of gendered racism leads to the creation of a racial enclave economy.

Chapter 2 offers a history of black women's work in the hair industry and reviews their participation in this industry in the present day. I discuss the historical contexts that pushed black women into employment and entrepreneurship in this field. I also describe the present-day black hair industry. This chapter thus situates black women's current entrepreneurship in the hair industry in historical context.

Chapters 3, 4, and 5 explore the black hair salon as an example of a racial enclave economy. These chapters detail the ways in which gendered racism has produced a context that shapes black women's entrepreneurial work in the hair industry, thus creating this racial enclave economy. Systemic gendered racism creates a racial enclave economy by playing a key role in shaping black women's entrepreneurial decisions, motivations, and relationships with employees in the hair salon. Chapter 3 describes how gendered racism creates an available market and contends that knowledge of this market guides black women's decisions to become and remain entrepreneurs in the hair industry rather than in other fields. Chapter 4 argues that gendered racism shapes these women's occupational opportunities such that entrepreneurship in the hair industry becomes a financially lucrative option. Finally, chapter 5 explores not only the emergence of racial, gendered, and class solidarity among owners and workers as a response to systemic gendered racism, but also considers how gendered racism is, paradoxically, replicated in the salon.

In chapter 6, I examine ethnic differences among black women salon owners in order to explore ethnic diversity within the racial enclave economy. Though the central tenet of this book is that black women's entrepreneurship in the hair industry constitutes a racial enclave economy, the racial label "black" includes various ethnic groups—Jamaican, Haitian, Ghanaian, Ethiopian, among others, and even some darker-skinned Cubans, Puerto Ricans, and Dominicans may be classified and treated as black regardless of their ethnic background. Consequently, this chapter focuses on African woman immigrants who are salon owners, in order to determine whether and how their encounters with systemic gendered racism create a different experience in the racial enclave economy.

Chapter 7 concludes the book by summarizing key points and discussing implications of entrepreneurship in the racial enclave economy. Like the patterns of ethnic entrepreneurship that are frequently the subject of research, the racial enclave economy is multifaceted and complex. In this chapter, I consider some of the paradoxes, challenges, and contradictions that arise from black women's entrepreneurial work in the racial enclave economy. I conclude with governmental policy implications and practices.

CHAPTER ONE

Introducing the
Racial Enclave Economy

Race and Ethnicity

Focusing on the experiences of black women entrepreneurs necessitates an emphasis on race rather than ethnicity. Though often used interchangeably, race and ethnicity denote two conceptually distinct categories. When discussing race, sociologists refer to the obvious physical characteristics common to a group. *Ethnicity* refers to the cultural or national origin of a group. Thus, there are many more ethnicities than there are racial groups. In contemporary America, racial groups are recognized as Asian American, Latino, black American, white, or Native American. Yet within these racial groups a multitude of ethnicities coexist, often with dissimilar cultural and historical backgrounds. Race and ethnicity are thus related concepts, but are not synonymous. According to American racial classifications, Japanese, Koreans, Chinese, Hmong, and Cambodians are all considered Asian, though these ethnic groups hail from different countries, speak different languages, and have distinct histories (some of which include inter-ethnic conflict).

Thus, conflating ethnicity with race presents a particular problem. Ethnic groups' experiences are often shaped by their particular cultural history and background. The background of one ethnic group may be quite distinct from another, even when they are both considered members of the same racial groups. These diverse ethnic backgrounds can produce radically different outcomes and experiences, even among ethnic groups that share a racial affiliation. For instance, both Koreans and Cambodians are ethnic groups that would be racially categorized as Asian American. Yet to focus on high achievement and academic success among Korean students obscures the fact that Cambodians, Hmong, and other southeast Asian ethnic groups often struggle academically.[1] Understanding the experiences of Korean American students does not necessarily imply a broader assessment of Asian American students' academic performance. Ethnicity is not a substitute for race.

These differences become even more evident with comparisons across ethnic and racial groups. In keeping with the example of educational achievement, Korean American students often demonstrate high levels of academic success.[2] Yet Korean Americans' educational success does not facilitate comparisons to other racial groups like American Indians or Latinos. In other words, exploring the various causes that may contribute to high rates of academic achievement among Korean Americans does not permit generalizations to racial groups. We may argue that Korean Americans succeed in school because of positive peer group reinforcement, socioeconomic status, a combination of these, or other factors. But the experiences of Korean Americans, as an ethnic group, are not synonymous with the experiences of racial groups. Again, ethnicity is not equivalent to race.

Systemic Racism as a Theoretical Tool for Understanding Racial Discrimination

Noting that race and ethnicity are conceptually distinct categories, sociologists have devoted a great deal of attention to theoretical and empirical research on race. Thus, a number of useful theoretical frames have been advanced as a means of understanding race and racism in America. Racial formation theory argues that race is a principle of social organization that shapes interactions at the micro and macro levels.[3] Further, the state plays an important part in how racial meanings are transformed and contested. Specifically, negotiations at the state level inform how racial categories are created, which then affects how race becomes part of interaction between individuals at the micro levels and how race becomes embedded in political, economic, and social systems at the macro levels. While the racial formation perspective heavily emphasizes the role of the state in creating racial categories, this framework offers an important focus on race as a social structure.

A more recent theoretical paradigm for understanding race and racism is the colorblind perspective.[4] This framework suggests that there is a racialized superstructure wherein races are hierarchically ranked. Within this superstructure, racial inequality is maintained through a combination of ideology and practice. The ideologies and practices that create racial inequality constitute a racialized social system. Racialized social systems are fluid and malleable, altering to reflect political and social changes. In the post–Civil Rights era, the ideology of racial colorblindness masks the pervasive ways in which racial inequality is perpetuated and continued. Colorblind racism enables whites to ignore processes of inequality that advantage them while simultaneously supporting policies and behaviors that perpetuate inequality.

While both of these theoretical frameworks offer useful conceptual tools for thinking about racism, I use the theory of *systemic racism* to assess the ways that race, rather than just ethnicity, shapes the entrepreneurial experiences of certain groups.[5] This perspective puts racism into historical context, focusing on its constancy and embeddedness in all aspects of U.S. society. This historicism is useful for understanding the broader context of black entrepreneurship and how the present state of this entrepreneurship owes a great deal to historic racism. The systemic racism frame argues that U.S. society is a racist whole comprised of a complex network of interconnected social institutions, ideologies, organizations, and other parts. These various interacting parts of the whole perpetuate racist oppression. As such, American society is one in which racial oppression exists as a systemic, core aspect of its general functioning. Within this society, "white on black oppression is systemic and has persisted over several centuries without the broad and foundational racial transformations that many social analysts suggest should have happened."[6]

One of the most important dimensions of systemic racism has to do with its role in constructing and legitimizing the economic exploitation of blacks by whites. From the seventeenth century onward, whites have been complicit or directly involved in appropriating the economic rewards of black labor. This appropriation began with slavery, continued as blacks were relegated by legal segregation into low-wage labor, and is manifested in the present day where comparisons between median incomes and levels of wealth routinely show blacks as lagging behind whites. Thus, a key component of systemic racism is the ideological support for and institutionalized practice of black economic exploitation, of which whites are the beneficiaries. Since an important part of systemic racism is the assertion that racial exploitation is inherent in U.S. social systems, it is important to consider how black exploitation is an intrinsic part of American economic systems.

The economic exploitation by whites of racial minority groups, particularly blacks, has a long and well-documented history in the United States.[7] The foremost example of black economic exploitation as a legitimate facet of the American economic system is found in the institution of slavery. During this time period, any black could be sold into slavery. The institution of slavery was specifically racialized in that only blacks could be enslaved. Even though not all whites owned slaves, not all blacks were slaves, and a small minority of blacks even owned slaves, the racial hierarchy clearly established that only blacks were eligible for this brutal system of servitude.[8] Consequently, whites were able to keep the economic rewards of the labor performed by blacks, which allowed whites to establish intergenerational transfers of wealth and to bolster the economy of many slave states and ultimately the entire nation. Even whites who did not own slaves benefited not only from the psychological advantage of being considered socially superior to another group, but also from reduced competition for jobs and education. This institution was buttressed by other social systems, including the legal and judicial systems, as evidenced by the Supreme Court's 1857 ruling in the *Dred Scott v. John F. A. Sandford* case, in which Chief Justice Taney ultimately ruled that a black person had no rights that a white man was bound to respect.[9]

Systemic racism was implicated in the economic exploitation of blacks during the antebellum periods, as well. During legal segregation, blacks were generally denied access to occupations and educational opportunities that facilitated social and economic mobility. Segregation ensured that whites had access to any colleges, jobs, and work that they could afford to pursue. In contrast, blacks were relegated to the lowest rung of the economic ladder. Concrete effects of this are evident in the types of occupational positions in which blacks were overrepresented: domestic work, sharecropping, tenant farming, and other low-wage service jobs. These labor market patterns benefited whites by reducing competition for jobs and establishing access to higher wages. Additionally, "much greater economic opportunities and assets meant better access for whites in many housing, educational, or political opportunities or assets."[10]

It is important to contrast here the ways systemic racism affected blacks and how the absence of this institutionalized, legitimate discrimination affected other ethnic groups that voluntarily migrated to the United States around this time. The late 1800s and early 1900s were a time of increased immigration, where white ethnics were able to capitalize on educational and economic opportunities to experience socioeconomic mobility and assimilate into mainstream society. Italian, Irish, German, and other white ethnic immigrants faced discrimination during this time period but were not subjected to the more extreme systemic racism that marked them as members of an inferior racial group. These white ethnics could exercise voting rights and therefore could access the political system, and—despite constraints—enjoyed far greater freedom within the labor market than did blacks. Since these white ethnics did not have to confront systemic racism, in that funda-mental way, their experiences—entrepreneurial and otherwise—differed from those of black Americans. (This further underscores the fallacy of con-flating ethnicity with race.)

In contemporary times, systemic racism still has a sizable impact on the economic position of black Americans. Numerous studies detail the chal-lenges blacks face in the labor market, from employer discrimination to glass ceilings to outright or covert racial harassment.[11] As a consequence of the continuing nature of systemic racism, blacks are overrepresented in low-wage sectors of the labor market that offer scarce potential for economic stability. Even blacks in professional occupations contend that racism remains an ob-stacle to upward mobility, impeding access to social networks that facilitate advancement and leading potential customers, coworkers, and supervisors to doubt their capabilities and professional acumen.[12] As in the past, whites benefit directly from these exclusionary processes in the form of increased ac-cess to more lucrative jobs, enhanced wages, and minimized competition. For blacks, the consequences of contemporary economic exploitation include less access to wealth, economic stability, and quality health care, not to men-tion increased stress.[13]

Systemic racism is legitimized through the use of frames. These frames shape the ways social actors perceive themselves, racial "others," and various social institutions and issues. Racial frames are fluid and are influenced by historical context, but the systemic racism perspective argues that racial frames have remained remarkably consistent over time, and ultimately the dominant racial frames work to justify racial inequality and white-on-black oppression. According to this framework, then, the commonly articulated white racial frame of the Jim Crow era argued that whites were inherently su-perior to blacks, who needed to be segregated from white society and to "know their place" as an inferior race. In the post–Civil Rights era, the dom-inant white racial frame downplays the theme of inherent inferiority, but still suggests that blacks suffer from cultural deficiencies that render them lazier, more prone to complaining and seeking handouts, and more averse to hard work than whites.[14] Throughout history, the dominant white racial frame has included "negative prejudices, stereotypes, images, ideas, notions, propensi-ties, interpretations, and action orientations that whites use to make sense of the world around them."[15]

In addition to the dominant racial frames that are used by whites to ra-tionalize racial hierarchies, the systemic racism framework also argues that black counterframes help black Americans to resist the negative racial mes-sages embedded in the dominant racial frames of systemic racism. Less work has been done on this in sociological circles, but black counterframes often incorporate close scrutiny of institutional structures that are used within dominant racial frames to legitimize inequality. Thus, blacks may adopt a counterframe that allows them to critique messages of black inequality by focusing on the ways various institutions (media, schools, labor markets) facilitate blacks' unequal position in society.

It is important to point out that while these frames and counterframes exist, they do not essentialize race. Not all whites employ the dominant white racial frame; not all blacks make use of black counterframes. Research does indicate, however, that blacks are more likely to develop and employ counterframes than to buy into dominant white racial frames that suggest their inferiority.[16] But even with counterframes, blacks are still susceptible to the messages of the dominant white racist frame. As the systemic racism framework indicates, the dominant white racist frame is embedded in and promoted by most social institutions (which are owned and controlled by whites). As such, this frame is more widespread and has greater influence than do black counterframes. Thus, blacks may accept the messages of the dominant white racial frame, endorse those of black counterframes, or alternately interpret issues through the lens of one or the other (or both).

Systemic Gendered Racism

One important aspect of the theory of systemic racism is its attention to how gender mediates the ways black men and black women encounter racism. Within the structure of systemic racism, black women's racial oppression is further complicated by virtue of their position as women. One of the most painful examples of how systemic racism is gendered involves the frequent occurrences of black women's sexual abuse and rape at the hands of white men. Up until the post–Civil Rights era, white men had virtually unrestricted sexual access to black women.[17] Consequently, black women, perhaps more than any other racial group, have a centuries-long history of nominal control over their reproduction. Indeed, as a result of the long-standing acceptability of white men's rape of black women, "it is likely that no other U.S. racial group's physical makeup has been so substantially determined by the sexual depredations of white men, which depredations took place for substantially more than half this country's total history."[18]

In this book, I build upon this analysis by developing the concept of *systemic gendered racism*. I contend that while systemic racism exists, it is a gendered system wherein race and gender are inextricably linked and overlapping, thus creating particular but not necessarily identical outcomes for minority men and minority women. Systemic racism refers specifically to the fundamental, centuries-long systems of white-on-black oppression in American society, and the idea that this oppression is foundational to U.S. society and continues over time to permeate its social institutions—media, political and economic systems, and public spaces. I argue that to conceptualize fully the nature of systemic racism, it is essential to consider how its manifestations are gendered, producing varied outcomes for the women and men who experience it.

The idea of gendered racism itself is not new. A number of feminist researchers have called attention to the fact that minority women experience disadvantage based on both race and gender, citing experiences in public settings, the labor market, various occupational spheres, religious institutions, and community organizing.[19] Afro-Dutch sociologist Philomena Essed was perhaps the first to introduce this term in her study of everyday racism, arguing that "gendered racism refer[red] to the racial oppression of black women as structured by racist and ethnicist perceptions of gender roles."[20] Though Essed's conceptualization of gender as an array of roles has been supplanted by more recent feminist scholarship situating gender as an achievement and later as an institution, her core idea that racism is gendered is the basis of my elaboration to the systemic gendered racism framework.[21]

In particular, the concept of systemic gendered racism owes a theoretical debt to multicultural feminist theory, which argues that women's experiences are best understood relative to their racial position. Systemic gendered racism, though, focuses on the historical, continuing systemic racism that is endemic to U.S. society, and argues that this racism is gendered in the ways that it impacts minorities. Aspects of systemic racism like the exploitation of racial minorities, political disenfranchisement of minority groups, and the legalized inequality of racial minorities are gendered. Thus, I emphasize social structures to argue that the racism embedded therein is gendered. By developing the idea of systemic gendered racism, I extend the theoretical and empirical work in this area to argue that inasmuch as racial oppression is continuing and fundamental to U.S. society, the "racial dimensions" like racist ideology, racist imagery, and racist institutions that allow systemic racism to flourish are gendered.

The concept of systemic gendered racism argues that the dominant white racial frames and competing counterframes are also gendered. Similarly, as frames are employed to legitimize (or challenge) systemic racism, I suggest that these frames are also gendered. The contemporary dominant white racist frame that associates criminality with blacks is a gendered racist frame. Black men are disproportionately associated with violent crime and are stereotyped as deviant criminals. This white racist framing is especially prevalent not only in the minds of whites who internalize this framing, but is also institutionalized and reproduced in the criminal justice and legal systems. Police brutality and racial profiling are examples of forms of violence that are frequently visited upon black and Latino *men* as a consequence of the gendered nature of this dominant white racist frame.[22]

Black counterframes to systemic racism are also gendered. Through social institutions like the mass media, systemic gendered racism depicts controlling images of black women that suggest that they are unable to meet the prevalent standards of femininity. In particular, black women are rarely able to conform to mainstream beauty ideals that idealize long, preferably blonde hair and light skin. The idea that black women are not really "women" has been used to justify their exploitation in the labor market and their subordination in other social settings.[23] This frame is gendered and racialized, as are the counterframes that challenge its messages. Though she does not use the specific terminology of the black counterframe, sociologist Patricia Hill Collins has argued that black women challenge these social messages through the development of broader, more inclusive ideals of beauty, often emphasizing inner strength over physical features. This way of thinking can be conceptualized as a counter-racist frame. It is important to note, though, that this counterframe is also specifically gendered, speaking to the particular experiences of black women in systemic racism.

Contemporary manifestations of systemic racism are also gendered. Schools are examples of social institutions where systemic racism is evident. Educational institutions disproportionately track black students into remedial or special education programs, minimize or marginalize minority experiences and contributions in school curricula, and often demonstrate faculty and institutional insensitivity to the particular experiences of minority children.[24] Yet the racialized ideologies and imageries that promote this institutionalized racism are gendered; black boys are seen primarily as either "criminals" or "endangered species," a set of controlling images that lead teachers to perceive these boys' behavior as aberrant and deviant, only to be "corrected" through treatment similar to that which is encountered in correctional facilities.[25] In contrast, black girls are seen by teachers as the ones who will have to lead their communities since "all the Black men are on drugs or in jail, or killing each other."[26] Systemic racism shapes the educational system in a way that marginalizes black children but does so through the use of gendered images, policies, and norms.

Systemic gendered racism has particular implications for black women's economic opportunities and their chances for economic stability. Past examples of systemic racism facilitating blacks' economic exploitation include slavery, constrained occupational opportunities under segregation, depressed wages, and, in the present day, workplace discrimination and lack of access to influential social networks. However, when we pay attention to the gendered nature of systemic racism, we see that, for black women, economic exploitation in these areas takes on a particular character. As previously discussed, systemic gendered racism meant that during slavery, black women's economic exploitation took the form of being raped by white men, often slave owners, in order to increase their capital. During segregation, systemic gendered racism meant that black women were limited to low-wage work, but this work was most commonly in the area of domestic service—a feminized area that conformed to patriarchal ideas that women were best suited for work in the home, as well as racist ideas that blacks were best suited for service work.

In modern times, systemic gendered racism renders black women subject to specific controlling images that legitimize their unequal treatment. In her analysis of controlling images and their role in perpetuating what she terms the "new racism," Patricia Hill Collins argues that black women are subjected to class-specific, gendered, controlling images that are used to justify a global racism disseminated through mass media.[27] Collins suggests that working-class black women are subjected to controlling images of the Bitch and the Bad Black Mother, while middle-class black women face controlling images of the Black Lady, educated Black Bitch, or Modern Mammy. One particularly important consequence of these controlling images is their function in justifying black women's depressed wages (particularly relative to black men and white men and women).

This is not to say that systemic gendered racism only impacts black women. The gendered nature of systemic racism affects other minority women as well. Yen Le Espiritu's important study of the ways race, gender, and class impact Asian Americans documents that immigration patterns were systematically racist in their exclusion of certain groups, especially the Chinese.[28] However, these racist practices were also gendered. Chinese men were encouraged to immigrate in order to fill low-wage labor positions, while Chinese women were either barred from entering the country or pushed into prostitution, given the absence of available employment opportunities.

The comparative examples of Asian and black women's experiences with systemic gendered racism underscore that this structure impacts minorities as a whole, but differently impacts men and women and various racial groups. Yet within systemic gendered racism, various race/gender groups are ordered so that while there are parallels across groups, there are still unique experiences that are applicable only to certain groups. Systemic gendered racism shapes economic structures like the labor market so that minority women are concentrated in low-wage labor—this is true for black women, Latinas, and Asian American women. Yet the economic exploitation of these women is not identical, such that systemic gendered racism is situational and is manifested differently across various groups.

Table 1.1 charts the systemic character of gendered racism and the ways it is embedded in social, economic, legal, and educational spheres. In the social sphere, gendered racism is manifested in controlling images of various race/gender groups. Thus, gendered racism in social arenas can be observed in part through media images of black women as bitches, mammies, and jezebels, or of black men as criminals, or of Asian American women as lotus blossoms or dragon ladies.[29] Gendered racism in the legal system constructs certain race/gender groups as criminals, so that Asian American men comprise a small percentage of those incarcerated, while black men constitute the majority. Similarly, gendered racism in educational spheres can encourage educational professionals to ignore Asian American students who need academic assistance out of the belief that they are "naturally" smart; in contrast to perceiving black male students as dangerous threats who benefit from strict, penal-style discipline.[30] Consequently, Asian American men outpace black men as college graduates.

These different groups' experiences are also hierarchically ranked. While systemic gendered racism impacts black men, black women, Asian American men, Asian American women, Latinos, and Latinas in ways that may be sim-

Table 1.1. Systemic Gendered Racism

Educational inequality (college graduation rates, highest to lowest)	Legal inequality (smallest to largest percent incarcerated)	Media (controlling images)
Asian American women	Asian American women	Asian American men → computer nerds, sexless sidekicks
Asian American men	Asian American men	Asian American women → Dragon ladies and Lotus blossoms
Black women	Latinas	Latinos → illegal immigrants
Latinas	Black women	Latinas → maids
Black men	Latinos	Black men → criminals
Latinos	Black men	Black women → bitches, mammies, jezebels

ilar but provide different outcomes for each group, this does not mean that their experiences are interchangeable. In a society structured by systemic gendered racism, certain race/gender groups may be considered more assimilable and acceptable to whites. Systemic gendered racism in the economic sphere may thus channel Asian American women into different occupations than black women. Unlike black women, however, the niches into which Asian American women are channeled are often white-collar, professional occupations where they are likely to have frequent contact with whites.[31] Systemic gendered racism in the labor market thus produces different outcomes for Asian American and black women, with Asian American women concentrated in more economically stable fields.

I contend that when systemic gendered racism is taken into consideration, the social, economic, occupational, and most importantly, entrepreneurial experiences of racial minority groups can be analyzed much more comprehensively. It becomes evident that the systemic nature of racism in American society is gendered and has a profound impact on racial groups' options, decisions, motivations, and behaviors in the workplace and on their status in the labor market. Consequently, systemic gendered racism has enormous implications for racial groups' entrepreneurial activity, but the connections between the two have been virtually ignored. The nature of racism as a gendered, systemic, and essential component of American society means that in order to understand the entrepreneurial experiences of racial groups, we must consider various aspects of systemic gendered racism on their entrepreneurial motivations, decisions, and outcomes.

Patterns of Ethnic Entrepreneurship

Despite important conceptual differences between race and ethnicity, much sociological research on entrepreneurship focuses primarily on the entrepreneurial experiences of ethnic groups. The most commonly identified patterns of ethnic entrepreneurship are *middleman minority* and *ethnic enclave entrepreneurship*. *Middleman minority* theory claims that ethnic entrepreneurs establish businesses where they function as intermediaries between elites and masses. In these businesses, they perform services that are necessary but hold low status and are therefore unappealing to elites. Historical examples of middleman minority businesses might include a rent collector or moneylender, while contemporary examples of middleman minority businesses might include a Chinese-owned dry-cleaners or a Korean-owned liquor store.[32] These small businesses are usually in "specialized occupational niches" that rely on contact with the broader society.[33]

However, this contact with the larger society is often a source of friction for middleman minorities. Many examples of the tension between Asian American (usually Korean) entrepreneurs and African Americans are attributed to the latter's resentment at the former's presence in predominantly black communities. Former Atlanta mayor Andrew Young was widely criticized for decrying the substandard yet high-priced goods Asian entrepreneurs sell in black neighborhoods: ". . . those are the people who have been overcharging us, selling us stale bread and bad meat and wilted vegetables. And they sold out and moved to Florida. I think they've ripped off our community enough. First it was Jews, and then Koreans, and now its Arabs . . . very few Black people own these stores."[34] However, Young's remarks underscored the frustration many blacks feel at the perceived ease with which Asian American immigrant entrepreneurs can own and operate businesses in black communities, as well as the disrespectful way blacks often feel they are treated by these entrepreneurs. The hostility here reflects a struggle that is not unique to these Asian American business owners, but one that is fairly common for middleman minority entrepreneurs.

Middleman minorities also maintain several important characteristics that differentiate them from other entrepreneurial groups. In applying the theory of middleman minorities to entrepreneurship, Bonacich argues that middleman minorities are first and foremost sojourners, with the explicit intention of residing in the host company only temporarily.[35] As these minorities always intend to return to the home nation eventually, they establish businesses that do not require a long-term commitment and will build enough capital to facilitate a return home. However, as sojourners, members of the host country may suspect that middleman minorities have divided loyalties and do not fully support the host country.[36] For instance, Chinese entrepreneurs turned to laundry work, which became an example of an ethnic enterprise that nicely suited their particular needs as middlemen minorities. Yet their economic success in this area does not eradicate the perception that Chinese (and Asian Americans in general) constitute an inassimilable minority.[37]

Additional arguments suggest that middleman minorities are also unique in their adherence to specific cultural traits that ensure their status as middleman minorities regardless of context or location. These studies point to Jewish, Chinese, and Indian entrepreneurs, arguing that these groups carry the label of middleman minorities in various societies.[38] These groups are thus seen as culturally predisposed to middleman minority status, in that "this historical continuity is generally accepted as an indication of the cultural heritage of middleman minority groups."[39] Cultural values, then, are cited as an explanation of some middleman minorities' entrepreneurial patterns and their success as business owners.

A key theme that has often been emphasized in the study of middleman minorities relates to how the issues of ethnic solidarity and host society hostility are inextricably intertwined. In other words, as middleman minorities encounter hostility from the host society, this strengthens their sense of internal solidarity and compels them to draw from and rely on support from co-ethnics. While some debate the extent to which ethnic solidarity facilitates immigrants' success in the ethnic economy, there is little research to suggest that middleman minorities do not experience hostility from various parties in the host society.[40] The reliance on internal solidarity has been documented among Korean immigrant middleman minority entrepreneurs in particular.[41]

In contrast to middleman minority businesses, *ethnic enclave entrepreneurship* is described as spatial concentrations of a variety of minority-owned firms that normally employ co-ethnics. The specific criteria for ethnic enclaves are that they must include a number of ethnically owned firms—though owners do not necessarily have to reside in the enclave—and that they employ co-ethnics. Unlike middleman minority enterprises, ethnic enclave economies often rely on their particular knowledge of co-ethnics' unmet business needs and desires. Thus, businesses in the ethnic enclave may serve ethnic foods or cultural products. They are able to capitalize on the existence of a protected market—co-ethnics' particular needs that are likely to be unmet by the larger, general economy. As such, ethnic enclave economies usually service a diverse customer base that includes co-ethnics, as well as the general public.

Alejandro Portes and his coauthors are credited with developing the entrepreneurial framework of the ethnic enclave, described thoroughly in Portes's research on Cuban entrepreneurs in Miami.[42] Portes and his collaborators argue that the migration patterns of Cuban immigrants helped to facilitate an ethnic enclave in the Miami area. Examining successive waves of Cuban immigrants, they suggest that earlier immigrants relied on capital brought from Cuba to establish businesses in retail trade, business, and repair sectors of the economy.[43] These business owners were then able to rely on co-ethnic solidarity to staff their labor force, employing even more recent Cuban immigrants in their business enterprises. Within this economic arrangement, salaried workers were found to earn the least, while self-employed workers with no employees earned more, and self-employed entrepreneurs with employees earned the most.[44]

One of the most important contributions of the ethnic enclave literature is its attention to whether ethnic enclave economies are inherently exploitative. Portes's work demonstrates that participation in the ethnic enclave allows ethnic employees to earn higher wages than they would in the general economy. Rather than being exploitative arrangements that take advantage of employees, these businesses rely on a pool of co-ethnics for employee labor, but also enable co-ethnic employees to become familiar with entrepreneurship so that they eventually can become business owners themselves. Other research has also suggested that women's participation as spouses and family members is crucial to the economic stability and success of the ethnic enclave economy.[45]

Middleman minority and ethnic enclave economies thus reveal distinctly different types of ethnic entrepreneurship. Middleman minorities serve the masses in petit bourgeoisie ventures and are often sojourners. Ethnic enclave entrepreneurs share a spatial concentration with other co-ethnics and experience split labor markets. However, these forms of ethnic economies share certain similarities. Both benefit from co-ethnic solidarity in their labor force, both service a multiracial customer base, but more importantly, both types of ethnic entrepreneurship are generally considered pathways to economic stability for ethnic immigrant groups. Portes and Bach specifically demonstrate the financial advantage co-ethnics can accrue in the ethnic enclave, and Bonacich suggests that middleman minorities are able to earn enough through their entrepreneurial activity to return to their homelands.[46] These frames have clearly been useful in understanding the entrepreneurial experiences of some groups, particularly Korean immigrants in California, Japanese immigrants, Cuban immigrants in Miami, and Chinese immigrants in various Chinatowns.[47]

Yet while these studies pinpoint characteristics of ethnic groups that enable them to engage in entrepreneurship (cultural capital, rotating credit associations), the focus on ethnicity precludes analysis of the larger racial group. In other words, the analysis of Korean and Japanese immigrants does not tell us, at large, about the experiences of Asian Americans as entrepreneurs. Too many groups are excluded—Cambodians, Filipinos—who have lower rates of entrepreneurship and whose experiences go unexplored when the focus is on ethnicity rather than race. The emphasis on ethnicity identifies particular patterns among these specific groups. A focus on ethnicity is not useful for addressing broader patterns that affect racial groups as a whole.

This preoccupation with ethnic groups' entrepreneurial activity is perhaps the most dangerous because it consequently ignores or minimizes the effect of racial discrimination in entrepreneurship. Though ethnic groups can and often do experience discrimination as members of racial minority groups, a focus on ethnicity prohibits comparison between ethnic groups and racial groups. Entrepreneurship research that focuses on the experiences of ethnic groups like Japanese, Koreans, Cubans, or Chinese cannot be generalized to address how institutionalized racism affects the entrepreneurial work of racial groups like blacks or American Indians. This is not to say that ethnic groups do not experience racial discrimination. The singular focus on ethnicity, though, offers limited means for addressing the ways ethnic groups are subjected to racialized mistreatment, and is even less useful for explaining the racialized (mis)treatment of various groups. In other words, the study of Chinese entrepreneurs does not necessarily illuminate racial mistreatment that Asian Americans may face as entrepreneurs. This focus also offers no framework for assessing racial barriers Asian Americans may face as entrepreneurs relative to those experienced by black Americans. With a systematic focus on racial groups' entrepreneurial activity, however, a broader understanding of entrepreneurial work is accessible.

Using Ethnicity to Explain Race: Blacks in the Ethnic Entrepreneurship Literature

The preoccupation with ethnicity rather than race has contributed to a bias in ethnic entrepreneurship literature. One way in which this bias is manifested is in the overemphasis on the factors, motivations, and processes that facilitate ethnic groups' entrepreneurship and the general inattention to how these causes may differently structure racial groups' efforts at business ownership. This is exemplified in the way studies of entrepreneurship suggest that racial groups' patterns of business ownership are somehow lacking or underdeveloped because they do not fit the models of entrepreneurship established by different ethnic groups. Too much of the research on black Americans and entrepreneurship reveals this predisposition.

While the middleman minority and ethnic enclave structures are the most commonly applied theoretical frameworks used for understanding ethnic economies, racial groups will not necessarily employ one of these patterns when engaging in entrepreneurship. Thus, when their entrepreneurial activity does not resemble the middleman minority and ethnic enclave paradigms, it is often overlooked in the literature. These omissions may be further exacerbated by the fact that when comparing racial groups' entrepreneurship to ethnic groups, the latter often have much higher numbers of entrepreneurial activity than the former. Korean, Chinese, and Cuban immigrants are among the most entrepreneurial groups; African Americans are among the least.[48] Researchers then often confine their study of black entrepreneurship to efforts to explain why blacks engage in entrepreneurship at lower rates than these other groups.

For instance, most researchers argue that variations in ethnic entrepreneurship can be explained by differential access to resources. In their study of ethnic groups' entrepreneurship, Light and Gold explain resource disadvantage as the absence of the skills and reserves necessary to facilitate entrepreneurship: "groups experience resource disadvantage when, as a result of some historical experience, such as centuries of slavery or peonage, their members enter the labor market with fewer resources than other groups."[49] The consequences of resource disadvantage are considered especially significant, as they prevent groups from having the essential resources that would enable them to engage in entrepreneurship as an alternative to the labor market disadvantage that clearly does exist.

This theory has been applied to explain inconsistent entrepreneurial participation among minority groups and low numbers of entrepreneurship among blacks in particular. Groups with more resources like "human capital, a positive work ethic, good diets, reliable health, contact networks, self confidence, and education" are better equipped to engage in entrepreneurial activity and consequently better represented among minority business owners.[50] Most studies indicate that these resources are available to many Asian and white-ethnic immigrants, thus explaining their greater participation as entrepreneurs in ethnic economies. In contrast, the most resource-disadvantaged groups are "blacks, Mexicans, Central Americans, [and] Hmong."[51]

Resource disadvantage theory draws important attention to the ways in which black entrepreneurs were denied access to the important and necessary resources that allow for successful entrepreneurship. Yet it fails to acknowledge any distinction between the structural, institutional processes by which blacks (as a race) are denied resources and the ways in which ethnic groups experience difficulty accessing resources. This theory does not take into consideration that institutional racial discrimination establishes barriers to resources that ethnic groups may not face. Light and Gold go so far as to assert that native-born whites may also experience discrimination based on age, sexuality, gender, or other factors.[52] While native-born whites may indeed experience discrimination in these areas, Light and Gold ignore the fact that native-born whites escape the pervasive *racial* discrimination that minorities face. In fact, as other researchers have shown, whites actually benefit from this discrimination in the forms of increased employment opportunities, greater access to wealth, and better educational opportunities for children.[53] Light and Gold's suggestion that the resource disadvantage faced by native-born whites can match or exceed that faced by racial minorities shows how the realities of race and racism have been glossed over in resource disadvantage theory.

Other research argues that even without comparisons to ethnic groups, black entrepreneurship is simply underdeveloped. This tradition of scholarship views black entrepreneurship as a "myth." Noted sociologist E. Franklin Frazier was one of the first and most vociferous proponents of this perspective. In his classic work, *Black Bourgeoisie*, Frazier argued that black businesses were unable to provide substantial contributions to the general American economy, nor were they able to offer sizable employment or significant income opportunities for the majority of blacks.[54] This view has been echoed in many later works that suggest that black businesses offer so little contribution to the general economy as to be generally irrelevant.[55]

It is certainly true that black Americans have been denied numerous resources that have contributed to their disadvantage in the United States. Unrestricted access to resources such as education, economic capital, social networks, and other assets might well have led to an increase in black entrepreneurship that could possibly have countered the disadvantage experienced in the occupational sector. Similarly, while a record of black entrepreneurship exists that dates back to the nineteenth century, this tradition of business ownership has not been a sizable source of jobs for other blacks nor has it been able to compete with mainstream American financial centers.

Yet while there is some truth to these arguments, it is also important to consider that they omit crucial factors that affected black business owners' entrepreneurial activity. In his study of black entrepreneurship, Butler offers an incisive critique of the flaws in the "myth of black entrepreneurship" literature, pointedly arguing that while black businesses may not be able to compete with larger, mainstream American financial centers, this fact is essentially true of most, if not all, forms of ethnic entrepreneurship.[56] Butler suggests that middleman minority and ethnic enclave economies likewise do not pose any challenge to American corporate and financial institutions, so to suggest that this is a flaw specific to black businesses is simply inaccurate.

Furthermore, Butler asserts that black entrepreneurial activity must be understood in the context of the specific disadvantage faced by this group. Not only does he take the resource disadvantage blacks have experienced into consideration, Butler argues that this disadvantage can be best understood in the context of a theoretical framework that explores the challenges oppressed groups face in capitalist economies. He suggests that "when the Afro-American business experience is placed within a comparative theoretical framework, the accomplishments of this group emerge in a positive light."[57] In other words, when the extent and scope of racial hostility and oppression are taken into consideration, black Americans' entrepreneurial work takes on particular significance.

With the realities of racial oppression in mind, Butler argues that certain patterns of black entrepreneurship actually resemble the middleman minority paradigm. Butler claims that the long history of black entrepreneurship indicates that there is a tradition of black Americans who have engaged in entrepreneurial activity as a reaction to American racism and discrimination. Taking these realities into account, Butler suggests that the structural inequalities produced by racism prevented black Americans from fully embodying all the characteristics of middleman minority entrepreneurs. He thus refers to this group as the truncated Afro-American middleman, arguing that they resemble other middleman minorities, specifically Jewish people in Europe and Japanese in California.

Using extensive historical data, Butler argues that the truncated Afro-American middleman holds specific values and ideals that are intrinsic to middleman minorities. He cites these as the emergence of internal solidarity (specifically manifested in the creation of community institutions) as a response to the larger society's aggression and hostility; the emphasis on creating stable family structures; and the importance of higher education as a route to upward mobility.[58] The truncated Afro-American middleman strongly influences the beliefs, values, and goals of the next generation, who become the "new middle class." This middle class has internalized the self-help values espoused by their entrepreneurial parents. As such, they appreciate cultural institutions in the black community and, like other offspring of middleman minority parents, are more likely to seek work in the skilled professions as doctors, lawyers, and professors, rather than to continue to engage in entrepreneurship.

Butler makes an extremely important theoretical contribution in examining the sociohistorical context in which blacks engaged in entrepreneurship. His work is one of very few that attempts to take into consideration the extent to which racial oppression shapes black entrepreneurs' work. He draws attention to the fact that social constraints established by government, economic institutions, and white citizens had an enormous restraining effect on blacks' entrepreneurial activity, and forcefully argues that studies of black entrepreneurship that do not take this history into consideration are remiss. Segregation alone limited black entrepreneurs' customer base to other black Americans, effectively slashing the available market. Economic institutions' refusal to loan money to aspiring black entrepreneurs (while lending to white ethnic groups) further hindered black business owners.[59] Finally, it is important to recall the social context in which black entrepreneurs attempted to thrive. Prominent business districts that were able to grow despite societal constraints of institutional racism were, in some cases, destroyed by whites.

The sociohistorical context in which blacks lived had a profound impact on all aspects of their lives, including their entrepreneurial experiences. This context must be taken into consideration when comparing black entrepreneurial activity to those of other groups.

Butler's work is very important because it draws attention to the realities of racism and discrimination that shaped black business ownership. Yet he still overlooks ways that institutionalized racism and discrimination affected certain groups of black entrepreneurs. His analysis leaves no room for understanding the experiences of contemporary working-class blacks who engage in entrepreneurship. According to Butler, these business owners are not descendants of the truncated Afro-American middleman and so have not benefited from the tradition of self-help that was handed down from this group through generations. What then explains why and how working-class blacks become entrepreneurs? Furthermore, the theory of the truncated Afro-American middleman does not explain how black entrepreneurship is gendered. Nearly half of all black-owned firms are owned by black women, and these numbers continue to grow at a rapid pace.[60] What explains women's increasing representation among black entrepreneurs?

In this book, I offer a critical reinterpretation that seeks to explore the systematic constructs that facilitate black women's entrepreneurship. To do this, I build upon Butler's arguments about the uniqueness of the experiences of African Americans relative to other groups. Specifically, I argue that the experiences of blacks, as a *racial* group, are not identical to the *ethnic* groups who are commonly the subject of ethnic entrepreneurship research. As such, I contend that a theoretical framework that considers the realities of racism is essential for understanding the experiences of black entrepreneurs. Further, I suggest that such a framework must take gender into account to demonstrate fully the systematic forces that shape black women's entrepreneurial work.

In this study, I argue that black women's entrepreneurial decisions must be understood in the context of the systemic gendered racism they experience in American social institutions and in everyday social spaces. I further contend that such a perspective has largely been absent in ethnic entrepreneurship research because of the emphasis on ethnic men as business owners. I suggest that systemic gendered racism in the social and economic spheres sorts various groups (such as Latinas, black men, and Asian women) into different slots on a racial/gendered hierarchy. In the case of black women, they are sorted into a low spot on the hierarchy, leading to limited economic and social options. I argue that this channeling leads some black women to create what I term a *racial enclave economy*.

The Racial Enclave Economy

I define a racial enclave economy similarly to the existing concept of the eth-nic enclave economy. Portes et al. coined the ethnic enclave economy framework to describe clusters of ethnic economies in a concentrated spatial location that serve a variety of business needs.[61] Initially used to describe the entrepreneurial patterns of Cuban immigrants in Miami, ethnic enclave economies employ co-ethnics and may capitalize on the entrepreneur's "in-sider knowledge" of a protected market. In other words, businesses in the eth-nic enclave may make it a point to target co-ethnic clients by selling cultural items or specialty foods. Portes also suggests that paid work in the enclave is a nonexploitative arrangement that benefits both workers and entrepreneurs—business owners hire low-wage labor in the form of co-ethnic employees, and workers find employment that pays better than that outside the enclave. They also are able to learn useful strategies and information to facilitate their transition to entrepreneurship.

The racial enclave economy maintains some similarities to the ethnic en-clave economy. Like the ethnic enclave, a racial enclave economy is charac-terized by the presence of fellow minority group members as owners and em-ployees. Further, within the racial enclave economy, businesses may or may not be located in a concentrated area. Unlike the ethnic enclave, however, the racial enclave economy emphasizes the role of systemic gendered racism as a preeminent factor shaping the experiences of minority entrepreneurs. In the racial enclave economy, businesses may or may not cater to that group's particular, unique needs.

I have argued here that systemic racism is gendered, is embedded in the legal, political, social, and economic spheres, and creates different, hierar-chically ranked experiences for race/gender groups. Systemic gendered racism in the economic and social spheres provides a context that leads racial minorities to engage in entrepreneurship. Table 1.2 suggests connections be-tween gendered racism in economic and social spheres and possible racial en-clave economies of various race/gender groups. Note that the controlling im-ages and median incomes of some race/gender groups may facilitate the formation of racial enclave economies that bring them into greater contact with whites and are likely to accrue greater economic returns.[62]

I argue that racial enclave economies are created when racial minorities encounter systemic gendered racism in various social structures and these en-counters push them toward entrepreneurship. In these cases, I term these en-trepreneurial patterns racial enclave economies because they distinctly re-flect the particular realities of race rather than ethnicity. Businesses in the

Table 1.2.   Racial Enclave Economies

Racial/Gender Group	Gendered Racism in Social Spheres	Median Income in 2005	Racial Enclave Economies
Asian American men	Computer nerds, sexless sidekicks	$34,215	Convenience stores
Asian American women	Lotus blossoms, dragon ladies	$21,641	Nail salons
Black men	Criminals, sidekicks, athletes	$22,653	Barbering, music
Latinos	Illegal immigrants	$22,089	Food service
Black women	Bitches, mammies, jezebels	$17,631	Hair salons
Latinas	Maids, illegal immigrants	$15,036	Hair and beauty services

racial enclave economy share several important characteristics: (1) owners' business decisions are impacted by systemic gendered racism; (2) owners' other work options are minimized by the existence of systemic gendered racism; (3) there exists the simultaneous reproduction and contestation of aspects of systemic gendered racism; and (4) owners share the same racial classification but different ethnic backgrounds.

In this book, I argue that systemic gendered racism has created a racial enclave economy in the form of black women–owned hair salons. This racial enclave is intrinsically gendered, which shapes black women entrepreneurs' decisions, motivations, and behaviors as business owners. Finally, focusing on the racial enclave economy offers a way to focus on the experiences of working-class entrepreneurs, who are routinely overlooked in the literature.

I rely on in-depth interviews with twenty-three black women salon owners to make the case for black hair salons as an example of a racial enclave economy. In the interviews, the women discussed their work history, the factors that led them to the hair industry, and the motivators that compelled them to become entrepreneurs. They talked about the struggles and specific challenges that faced them as entrepreneurs in this field, along with the particular advantages and drawbacks of work in this area. Respondents also discussed sources of competition in the field and their long and short-term goals as entrepreneurs.

CHAPTER TWO

History of Black Entrepreneurship

Black Entrepreneurship during Slavery

Blacks have a long, rich history of business ownership dating, surprisingly, back to the days of slavery. Generally, it was free blacks who were able to establish businesses. These entrepreneurial ventures were established in a variety of fields including "merchandising, real estate, manufacturing, construction trades, [and] transportation."[1] In cities like New Orleans, Philadelphia, and Cincinnati, free blacks ran notable businesses in the service industry, with black entrepreneurs working as tailors, restaurateurs, caterers, sail-makers, and blacksmiths. Both whites and other free blacks were clients of these early entrepreneurs. Business ownership thus offered free blacks a way to achieve a degree of economic stability that was absent among wage-earning and enslaved blacks.

Of course, black entrepreneurs who established businesses during the days of slavery faced overwhelming obstacles along the way. Securing necessary capital was one of the most common challenges for these early black entrepreneurs. Blacks who were enslaved were not paid and generally dedicated what money they could make to purchasing their freedom and that of their loved ones. Free blacks generally were employed in low-wage jobs that did not pay well enough to establish the necessary economic capital for business ownership. Finally, banks and other funding institutions generally refused to loan money to blacks, although they would loan money to whites and white ethnic groups.[2] To address these inequities, blacks established mutual aid societies and established businesses in money lending.[3]

In addition to the banking systems, other white-controlled institutions threatened the success of black entrepreneurs. The machinery of the state functioned to limit black business by passing restrictive laws that curtailed blacks' mobility and rights and set a legal foundation for maintaining blacks' unequal status. As the highest judicial body in the land ruled that blacks had no rights that a white man was bound to respect, the stage was set for an up-hill battle for black entrepreneurs. Furthermore, since the law of the land was designed to render any black eligible for slavery, the constant threat of en-slavement shaped even free blacks' opportunities for business ownership. In some cases, laws were enacted that specifically restricted blacks' entrepre-neurial options, such as the decree that blacks could not obtain patents—thus limiting their opportunities to become self-employed as inventors.[4]

Competition from white entrepreneurs was another serious problem for blacks who attempted to own businesses during slave times. White entrepre-neurs resorted to numerous tactics to ensure that black entrepreneurs did not become too economically successful or present too serious a threat to their profits. These tactics ranged from undercutting prices to simply destroying black entrepreneurs' businesses.[5] Arguably, difficulties generating capital and establishing a business posed more immediate threats to black entrepreneurs than the hostility of white competitors, but it is important to point out that black business owners faced challenges at every turn.

In keeping with the central thesis of this book, the black entrepreneurship that did exist during slavery must be considered in light of the enormous ob-stacles these business owners encountered. Black entrepreneurs faced barri-ers that were specifically designed to oppress an entire racial group. From the state's insistence on relegating blacks to second-class citizenship to white in-stitutions' racial discrimination to white entrepreneurs' race-based resent-ment, black entrepreneurs faced racially specific challenges to entrepreneur-ship that were not presented to various ethnic groups. These impediments render black entrepreneurs' accomplishments during this time that much more impressive.

Entrepreneurship after Slavery

After slavery ended, prominent members of the black community debated the next step for blacks in what they hoped would be a more welcoming so-ciety. Noted intellectual and African American sociologist W. E. B. Du Bois argued that blacks should embrace culture and higher education, with an emphasis on voting rights as a crucial step toward integration. Du Bois theorized that with this focus, and with the top 10 percent of African

Americans responsible for uplifting less fortunate blacks—the talented tenth theory—blacks would eventually integrate into white society. His main rival at the time was Booker T. Washington, who advocated separation from white society, instruction in the skilled trades, and most importantly, entrepreneurship as a strategy for black advancement. For Washington, entrepreneurship was key to black economic mobility and to achieving civil rights. He felt that when blacks could gain economic stability independently of white institutions, they would have the financial standing that would enable them to improve their bargaining position in white-dominated society.

In modern times, Washington is often criticized as an accommodationist for failing to critique and, even to a degree, for embracing principles of segregation. Whatever one thinks of Washington's positions on integration, however, it is important to acknowledge that his embrace of entrepreneurship is a function of his assessment of the realities of capitalist society. Washington believed, possibly correctly, that with enough economic capital blacks would have to be treated more equitably by white society. Unfortunately, he underestimated the continuing significance of racism as a factor that would influence state policy, white violence, and social institutions, ultimately placing near-insurmountable restrictions on blacks' ability to secure this economic capital.

After the Civil War, blacks continued to engage in many of the same business enterprises as they had during slavery. However, the practice of racial segregation dealt an enormous blow to black entrepreneurs. During slavery, free blacks faced challenges to entrepreneurship in the form of laws intended to institutionalize their second-class status, which severely curtailed access to economic capital, and sometimes in the illegal tactics from white competitors. However, they had access to a racially integrated (though limited) market. The ability to service blacks and whites was very important for black entrepreneurs' economic success.

Racial segregation maintained and strengthened the challenges black entrepreneurs had faced during slavery. It also deprived them of their access to a multiracial customer base. This practice "was disaster for Afro-American business."[6] Segregation created an economic detour for blacks in the sense that governmental interference artificially condensed the available market. More importantly, this economic detour was racial, not ethnic. Ethnic groups—particularly white ethnics who are modeled as examples of hard work and eventual assimilation—never faced the economic detour to which black entrepreneurs were subjected. They were never forced by the state to limit the market for their services to co-ethnics only.

Butler writes at length on the distinction between what blacks, as a race, experienced compared to other ethnic groups:

> Despite the fact that different ethnic groups migrated to America and had an original period of difficulty, no other racial or ethnic group . . . has had to face the total and constitutionally sanctioned exclusion from the larger society that Afro-Americans have experienced. There have never been "German-only," "Irish-only," or "Italian-only" facilities. Despite the fact that sociologists have drawn interesting parallels between the Afro-American experience and that of European ethnic groups, the Afro-American experience stands in a different light. Put another way, the most divisive force in America has always been race, especially as regards black/white relations. . . . Europeans have spent a great amount of time excluding Afro-Americans from basic participation in the social and economic sector of America.[7]

The impact of this complete segregation and the economic detour it produced created a marked change in the history of black entrepreneurship. It crippled black entrepreneurs while simultaneously advantaging ethnic entrepreneurs who remained able to target the general market.

The economic detour, though devastating, did not eliminate black entrepreneurship completely. Rather, at this point, blacks recognized that the customs of segregation meant that whites would refuse certain forms of contact with blacks. They began to establish businesses to meet black customers' needs in these areas. This tenacity points to many blacks' faith in entrepreneurship as a way to establish economic stability despite tremendous odds. It also underscores the paucity of decent jobs and wages for blacks during this time, since many were driven to entrepreneurship not only out of natural business acuity but also out of a need to procure economic security.

Insurance, undertaking, and banking are examples of fields in which black entrepreneurship existed and, to a certain extent, flourished. Paradoxically, the success of these business ventures owes in part to the extensive racial discrimination and the resultant segregation that was widespread in the larger society. Insurance companies often would not insure blacks, claiming (ironically) that they were too high a risk given the substandard conditions in which they lived. Black entrepreneurs were able to fill this void, with some black business owners earning sizable fortunes in this field: "By 1932, Afro-Americans had established an insurance industry that was well organized and functional for the community."[8] Black entrepreneurs also established banks to address white-controlled banks' unwillingness to lend to black customers.[9] Finally, racial segregation literally extended beyond the grave—not only were cemeteries segregated, but white undertakers generally refused to work on black bodies. This led to the development of undertaking and funeral services as another niche available to black entrepreneurs.[10]

Two important and unique cases of black business development existed during this time. At the turn of the century, Durham, North Carolina, boasted a black business district eventually called Hayti that was especially noteworthy given its degree of support from wealthy whites and its ability to maintain white customers. With the North Carolina Mutual Life Insurance Company and the Mechanics and Farmers Bank anchoring the district, which included restaurants, theaters, grocery stores, and funeral parlors, Hayti became known as the Black Wall Street.[11] Remnants of that business district still exist, though desegregation and urban renewal have taken a toll on the area.

Tulsa, Oklahoma, like Durham, boasted a black business district that enjoyed an illustrious beginning. Unlike the black business district in Durham, Tulsa's Greenwood district met a disastrous end. Scholars have argued that a key part of the success of Hayti was the support it garnered from white elites at its inception. Greenwood began as a response to the economic detour blacks were forced to endure, but it lacked the cadre of supportive, wealthy whites as its champions. Consequently, as Greenwood flourished despite segregation, containing businesses in retail, food service, and other areas, white resentment steadily increased in response. In 1921, tensions erupted into a race riot, and during this riot the Greenwood district was destroyed. Greenwood was rebuilt into an even more impressive district, and did not begin to decline until urban renewal began to change the area and desegregation permitted blacks to patronize white businesses.

Contemporary Black Entrepreneurship:
The Post–Civil Rights Era

Social change during the late twentieth century dramatically affected the conditions surrounding black entrepreneurship. Perhaps the biggest changes stemmed from the gains of the Civil Rights movement, which resulted in an end to legal segregation and a shift in the way blacks were treated by most social institutions and in social settings in general. Integration and educational opportunity were perhaps the two outcomes of the Civil Rights movement that established the most drastic changes in black entrepreneurship.

The Civil Rights movement profoundly affected patterns of higher education among blacks. During segregation, most blacks who were able to attend college went to historically black colleges and universities. With integration, predominantly white institutions began to enroll the majority of college-bound blacks.[12] Along with access to predominantly white institutions came greater access to college-level study of business-related fields such as management, accounting, and finance before venturing into entrepreneurship. Formal study in this area is important, given that college-level training in these fields increases the likelihood that an entrepreneur will remain in business.[13]

As the stories of Greenwood and Hayti indicate, integration had an impact on black entrepreneurship, as well. When the yoke of segregation was lifted and blacks had greater choice in spending their consumer dollar, many opted to patronize white businesses. In other words, the protected market, which arose out of the economic detour to which blacks were subjected, disappeared. Insurance companies began to insure blacks, banks became willing to take their money, and undertakers consented to service black customers. Consequently, black entrepreneurs in these areas could no longer rely on the black community that could not get its needs met anywhere else.

On a related note, integration meant that more employment opportunities were available for blacks who, historically, might have pursued entrepreneurship for its financial possibilities. When the only occupational options available to blacks were enslavement or low-wage work, business ownership had been an attractive, though difficult, alternative. Conversely, integration offered blacks access to a wider variety of jobs in the general labor market. This increased blacks' opportunities, making entrepreneurship a less attractive option.

Once again, the changing landscape of black entrepreneurship does not mean that blacks stopped engaging in business ownership. On the contrary, the changes brought on by the Civil Rights movement facilitated more subtle and covert racist attitudes toward blacks. It became advantageous, in particular, for the state to move away from openly using the language of black inferiority and instead to employ rhetoric of creating equal opportunities for blacks. (Unfortunately, however, state policies that maintained blacks' status as second-class citizens remained in place even as representatives of this institution promoted racial equality.)

To this end, in the late 1960s, Richard Nixon was one of the main proponents of black capitalism, arguing that black business development was an important strategy for revitalizing black urban communities. For the first time in American history, federal funds were extended to black-owned businesses along with white ones.[14] This represents a major shift in the state's policies and attitudes toward black entrepreneurs. However, since that time, the vast majority of government money continues to go to white business owners, which limits the ability of black entrepreneurs to "achieve parity with white American businesses."[15]

As figure 2.1 indicates, black businesses today remain concentrated in the service industry. However, more blacks have begun to establish businesses in other fields, including construction and manufacturing.[16] Today, African Americans remain heavily involved in entrepreneurial activity, though racial disadvantage reproduces many problems similar to those endured by early black entrepreneurs—difficulty securing capital, problematic interactions with white competitors, and lack of unrestricted government support.[17]

As has always been the case, there are notable cases of black entrepreneurship that stand out even today. Perhaps one of the most impressive black entrepreneurs of today is Oprah Winfrey. Winfrey grew up poor in rural Tennessee but has managed to become a media mogul and is the richest black woman alive today. Winfrey's multimedia enterprises include a production company (Harpo), magazines (O, The Oprah Magazine, and O at Home), a radio network (Oprah & Friends), and a television network (Oxygen). Her success reflects some of the changes in black entrepreneurship, as she is able to access and relies on a racially diverse market and is an entrepreneur in the entertainment industry, rather than the service industry as was common to many black entrepreneurs of the past.

Distribution of Black-Owned Firms by Kind of Business: 2002
Total: 1,197,661

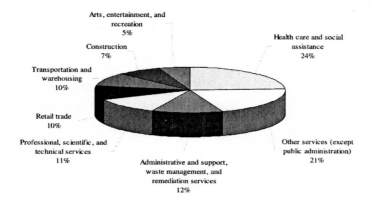

Note: Firms with more than one domestic establishment are counted in each industry in which they operated, but only once in the U.S. total.

Source: U.S. Census Bureau, 2002 Survey of Business Owners
Black-Owned Firms – Released April 18, 2006

Figure 2.1.

The music industry is another niche that has seen a dramatic increase in black entrepreneurship. Since the 1980s, several young, black men entrepreneurs have been able to develop lucrative businesses that began as music production companies and eventually branched out into clothing companies. Russell Simmons, CEO of Def Jam and Phat Farm enterprises, is one such entrepreneur who made his fortune marketing and producing hip-hop music in the 1980s and 1990s. Numerous other young black men followed suit, among them Sean Combs (better known as Puffy, Diddy, or P. Diddy), Percy Miller (known as Master P), and the most successful of all these entrepreneurs, Shawn Carter (known as Jay-Z).

The music industry represents an enormously significant area in the growth of modern-day black entrepreneurship. The cases of successful black entrepreneurs in this field are particularly interesting. While Simmons, Combs, Miller, and Carter sit at the helm of businesses worth several millions, none of these men have any formal business training and most did not even attend college.[18] Miller and Carter came from poor backgrounds in urban areas (New Orleans and Brooklyn, respectively) and both generated the economic capital to engage in entrepreneurship through their activity in the drug trade. Finally, like Oprah, these men market their products (music, sneakers, clothes, food) toward a multiracial mix of urban and suburban customers—but, tellingly, the music industry has not accepted black women entrepreneurs in the same ways that it has welcomed black men entrepreneurs. There is no woman in the music industry who is the entrepreneurial equivalent of Shawn Carter.

Systemic Racism as a Driving Force in Black Entrepreneurship

Looking over the history of black business ownership, several common themes emerge. The first is that the issue of economic detour had a profoundly important influence on the trajectory of black entrepreneurship. As Butler stresses, the practices of state-sanctioned segregation and artificial compression of the market were infringements placed only on blacks.[19] These restrictions were racialized and were not applied to ethnic groups who are commonly the subject of ethnic entrepreneurship literature. The importance of taking this context into consideration when studying blacks' entrepreneurial work cannot be overstated.

Secondly, the history of this economic detour continues to affect the entrepreneurial work of blacks even as segregation no longer remains a legally mandated doctrine. Blacks have only recently begun to move out of the service area and into other fields of entrepreneurship in large numbers.[20] The economic detour to which early black entrepreneurs were exposed means that modern-day blacks often lack the intergenerational transfers of wealth and economic capital that facilitate successful entrepreneurship.[21] In addition, the economic detour means that other ethnic groups that were able to escape these racialized decisions and social policy have outpaced blacks, creating an uneven playing field for black entrepreneurs.

Black business ownership, from its early onset to its contemporary manifestations, is thus best understood in the context of the systemic racism that characterizes U.S. society. Systemic racism in the occupational sector severely curtailed blacks' job opportunities, rendering their economic exploitation under slavery a "natural" part of American society. In response to this, free blacks engaged in entrepreneurship despite the hostilities they faced from systemic racism in the state and from white competitors. Systemic racism in the state and all other social institutions later mandated forced racial segregation, where blacks were not to utilize any of the same public facilities as whites. This created the economic detour that black entrepreneurs faced, wherein they were restricted to relying only on fellow blacks for their customer base. Black entrepreneurs responded to this form of systemic racism by establishing businesses intended to cater to black consumers' needs that were left untapped by segregationist policies. Finally, this systemic racism still has an impact on blacks' entrepreneurial ventures since they must now compete on a playing field which has excluded them for centuries.

Having reviewed the history of black entrepreneurship and explored how this history is best understood in the context of systemic racism, I turn now to examining the ways this history is gendered. Specifically, I look at the experiences of black women entrepreneurs in the hair industry to assess how the racialized context I described for black entrepreneurs was also gendered and had a particular effect on women. One consequence of systemic gendered racism for black women entrepreneurs is that these institutionalized forms of oppression play a role in leading them into entrepreneurship in the hair industry and shaping their decisions and behaviors once in this field.

Black Women Entrepreneurs in the Hair Industry

Though little scholarship focuses explicitly on their experiences, black women were very active in this tradition of black entrepreneurship. During slavery, free black women in the North and the South were engaged in a variety of entrepreneurial activities. Often these black female entrepreneurs were able to turn "gender-based domestic and manufacturing activities" into business enterprises, with women working as dressmakers, seamstresses, or midwives.[22] While most black female entrepreneurs of this time worked in the service or domestic industries (the vast majority were laundresses), black women owned and operated businesses in fields as diverse as banking and real estate.[23] Black female entrepreneurs established businesses in many of the same areas as men but most started businesses in traditionally "female" fields.

Black women's history of involvement in hair and beauty enterprises dates back to the days of slavery. In addition to sail-making, manufacturing, real estate, construction, and merchandising, hair and beauty ventures were one of many areas in which free blacks were able to develop entrepreneurial activity, limited though this activity was by legislation and the risk of re-enslavement. As early as 1838, the Pennsylvania business register lists hairdressers as the most populous entrepreneurial venture operated by black women.[24]

The black hair care industry began to flourish in the early twentieth century. This was connected to the fact that hair had become an increasingly prominent marker of status and beauty.[25] Most black women have dark hair that is naturally short and tightly curled. In many African cultures, black women ornately styled their hair, elaborately decorating it with beads, combs, and jewels. In American society, however, these styles and hair textures were depicted as unattractive and unsightly: "once Africans were brought to North America as slaves, hair was used to show humiliation, submission, and conformity."[26] Not surprisingly, as white women were idealized as the epitome of beauty, their hair textures, styles, and colors were glorified, while black women's natural hair textures, styles, and colors were vilified.

As the natural texture and length of black women's hair was construed as an indicator of their inferiority, a hair care industry designed to address issues of taming and straightening hair developed.[27] This industry sought to alleviate black women's struggles with their hair by selling do-it-yourself straightening products such as Black and White Ointment, Ozonized Ox Marrow, and Plough's Hair Dressing—all designed to reduce the natural coarseness and kinky textures of black women's hair. Initially, most of these companies were owned by whites who marketed products intended to turn "kinky, snarly, ugly, curly hair" to hair that is "soft, silky, smooth, straight, long, and easily handled, brushed, or combed."[28] Product advertisements promised that changing one's hair to the desired texture would "contribute to [one's] success—both socially and commercially."[29] These companies adopted notions of black Americans as inferior and unattractive for their marketing strategies, and professed that straight, smooth, long hair would in turn lead to social mobility, success, and, of course, beauty.

When black women began to develop, market, and advertise hair care products, their marketing strategies took a decidedly different slant. Several black women, including Madames Perkins, Smith, Newell, and Nelson, were notable entrepreneurs who sold hair care remedies designed to promote hair growth. In contrast to the marketing strategies of white companies, these women did not use rhetoric of racial inferiority to sell their products. They cited biblical passages extolling the virtue of long hair on women, used themselves as models to illustrate the success of their products, and, most importantly, emphasized potential career options for black women within the hair industry, often offering other black women work at their companies. In an effective marketing technique, Madame Annie Turnbo Pope Malone sent saleswomen who used her hair-growth product, Poro, door-to-door in black communities. These early entrepreneurs laid the groundwork for Madame C. J. Walker's business enterprise.

Madame Walker, inventor of the straightening comb, was arguably the most successful and the most well known of these black woman entrepreneurs in the hair care industry. Like Perkins, Smith, and the others, Walker refused to market her products in a way that reinforced black women's inferiority—she did not suggest that her products were necessary to counter ugly, kinky hair, nor did she proffer social mobility or happiness as a result of using her products. She instead argued that her products offered black women a healthy, workable way to grow their hair and to feel beautiful. Though Madame Walker did invent the straightening comb in 1905— different from the products of her predecessors because it "was one of the first that allowed African American women to change the texture of their hair consistently and make it straight"—she did not market this or any of her products as hair straighteners.[30] Instead, she preferred to market her products as a means to hair growth and developing black women's beauty and economic independence.

As the first black millionaire, Madame Walker achieved many successes, including her employment of numerous black women and remaining in business longer than many other similar companies.[31] One of her most important legacies is undoubtedly her emphasis on using the hair industry to create avenues for black women's economic independence, a goal she worked toward by employing black women. At the time of her death in 1919, Walker, at age 52, had ten thousand female employees and had stipulated in her will that her company be left to a woman. Her work pinpointing the hair care industry as a viable source for employment left a very distinct legacy.

It is important to acknowledge that many of Madame Walker's experiences, as well as her business enterprise, were profoundly shaped by intersections of gender and race. The fact that it was entrepreneurship in the hair industry that made her the first black millionaire of either gender reflects just how important hair issues were to black women. Also significant is Walker's emphasis that her entrepreneurial venture offered a pathway toward black women's economic stability. Her focus on helping women may well have been influenced by the sexism she experienced at the time—Walker rose to prominence during the time that Booker T. Washington was stressing the importance of business ownership as a route to economic independence for blacks after the Civil War. Yet, Washington failed to recognize Walker's obvious business savvy and even attempted to exclude her from the 1912 National Negro Business League Convention.[32]

A few years later, despite the dismal employment prospects that were commonplace during the Great Depression, many black women worked in the hair and beauty industry. In fact, as table 2.1 reveals, hair salons were among the most prevalent and profitable black-owned businesses of that time.[33] During this time, the beauty industry moved from door-to-door sales of do-it-yourself products to storefront or at-home salons. Analyzing data drawn from the 1940 Census and Indexes of Occupational Representation (IOR), Boyd suggests that in the urban North, the depressed economic conditions of the Depression actually led black women into the beauty culture business be-

Table 2.1. Mean Participation Rates (per 1,000 workers) of Black and White Women in Selected Occupations in Thirty-Four Northern Cities, 1940 (Standard Deviations in Parentheses).[a]

	Black Women	White Women
Laundry operatives and laundresses, except private family	34.05[b]	17.87
	(23.65)	(5.35)
Barbers, beauticians, and manicurists	23.25[c]	18.99
	(8.32)	(5.23)
Boarding house and lodging house keepers	22.32[b]	9.80
	(14.28)	(3.51)
Dressmakers and seamstresses, not in factory	11.02	12.44
	(5.73)	(3.29)
Proprietors, managers, and officials of eating and drinking places	4.19	4.15
	(3.09)	(2.18)
Proprietors, managers, and officials of retail stores	3.84[b]	14.43
	(4.67)	(3.50)
Canvassers, peddlers, and news vendors	.77[b]	1.98
	(.82)	(.76)

[a] Tests are two-tailed. Occupations are ranked by the means of black women.
[b] Black-white difference is significant, $p < .001$.
[c] Black-white difference is significant, $p < .05$.
Source: Robert Boyd, "Race, Labor Market Disadvantage, and Survivalist Entrepreneurship: Black Women in the Urban North during the Great Depression," 2000.

cause it provided rare avenues of employment, entrepreneurship, and even led to economic advancement for some salon owners: "beauty culture and hairdressing not only provided black women with opportunities for survivalist entrepreneurship, these occupations also helped some black women economically advance."[34]

Around this time, black entrepreneurship in the hair care industry also began to blossom in the beauty aids market. In a historical analysis of black entrepreneurial development in the beauty aids industry, Silverman cites the time between the Great Migration and the Great Depression as the period when the beauty aids industry (the manufacturing and sales of hair care products) began to emerge as a preeminent African American business institution.[35] Despite widespread poverty, black-beauty-aids manufacturers were able to remain in business during the Great Depression. The demand for beauty aids products came primarily from black women who were attempting to increase their attractiveness to potential employers in order to find much-needed work.[36] In addition, blacks were the only group involved in manufacturing black-beauty-aids products, so they had a virtual monopoly in the market. Though most beauty aids manufacturers were small- to medium-sized black-owned companies, they were able to profit because black owners understood the special needs of black customers and were able to create a product for those needs.

The social conditions that concentrated black entrepreneurs into limited occupations (such as barriers to education and racial segregation) changed with the Civil Rights movement. Though the hair care industry remained a field highly populated by black women, black entrepreneurs now had the option of exploring other, more lucrative fields. As black women's social disadvantage lessened during the 1960s and into the 1970s, they began to take the increasingly available clerical positions, with fewer exploring entrepreneurship in small business areas.[37] Additionally, the newly popularized "afro" hairstyle led some black female customers to renounce chemical straightening; profits in some salons were reduced as a result but the industry overall continued to profit well.[38]

Black women's participation in the hair industry reveals that entrepreneurial activity in this field has historically offered them a way to counter persistent economic disadvantage. These early entrepreneurs were able to achieve financial gain by establishing business enterprises where they styled and cared for black women's hair and sold hair care products.[39] They frequently created employment opportunities for other black women as well; as a result, black women were well represented in the hair care business. When the hair care industry first began to develop and expand, most of the black women involved in the business engaged in entrepreneurial activity by selling hair care products door-to-door or opening salons. As the industry progressed and continued to grow, black-female owned hair salons became more central to black women's participation and economic gains in this field.

Today, beauty salons constitute an important segment of black-owned businesses. Contemporary data on black women workers in the hair industry are extremely rare, but black women are estimated to comprise approximately 100,000 of about 300,000 women employed as stylists nationwide, with about 50,000 black women self-employed as salon owners.[40] A quick perusal of a website that catalogues black salon owners (www.hairweb.com) also revealed that a sizable number of them are owned by women. In one metropolitan area, the site lists seventy-five hair salons owned by blacks, 89 percent of which are owned by black women.

One reason black hair salons are so universal is that black women's hair care remains a lucrative market. Trends in the hair industry revealed that black female consumers are a profit-inducing market for hairdressers. Advanstar, the annual report on trends and changes in the hair industry, reported in its 2001 issue that 68 percent of salons offered relaxers (the chemical process used to straighten black women's hair), the average price of which is $42.00. Relaxing hair comprised 22 percent of all salons' weekly business, which indicates that African American women provided nearly a quarter of salons' weekly profits. Advanstar's 2002 issue indicated that the industry revenues from relaxers increased from $8.5 billion in 2000 to $8.7 billion in 2002. In 1999, ethnic hair care products and ethnic hair care services sold and performed in salons earned the industry $46.7 billion. Since African American women usually have their hair care needs served by other African American women, they constitute an important and valuable component of the hair industry as both stylists and customers.

The contemporary black hair salon, then, is especially important inasmuch as it has been and continues to be a mainstay of black women's entrepreneurial activity. Black hair salons continue to thrive, and continue to serve a rapidly growing and financially lucrative market. Many black women now have opportunities to attempt other forms of entrepreneurship and to follow avenues for economic mobility that, as a result of segregation and widespread discrimination, were once unavailable to black women. Although most black women entrepreneurs still remain in gender-typed fields, they are also found in the entertainment and financial industries.[41] In fact, there are a number of black women who take advantage of these opportunities and pursue high-paying careers or attempt entrepreneurship in other, less traditional fields, contributing to the steadily increasing numbers of black women entrepreneurs.[42] The fact remains, however, that despite increased occupational and entrepreneurial opportunities, the hair salon remains a popular form of business ownership for African American women.

Systemic Gendered Racism and Black Women's Entrepreneurship

Black women's history of entrepreneurial work in the hair industry thus represents the influence of systemic gendered racism. Historically, systemic racism meant that in virtually all social spheres, blacks were considered inferior to whites. Blacks' physical features—darker skin, fuller lips and noses—were, through the lens of systemic racism, presented as objectionable and considered an obvious testament to their inferiority. However, this systemic racism was also gendered in that it intersected with messages about femininity, which stated that women's worth was directly tied to their physical attractiveness. For black women, systemic racism became gendered; the physical features that were held up as a marker of their racial inferiority also precluded them from achieving dominant ideals of femininity. The natural state and texture of their hair was one of the key physical traits used to signify their racial inferiority and their lack of "true" femininity. The history of black women's work in the hair industry is linked to systemic gendered racist constructions of the social significance of hair.

Historically, systemic gendered racism meant that black women experienced economic exploitation as they were only considered eligible for the very worst jobs. Up until the social changes instituted by the Civil Rights movement, the most common job for black women was as domestic workers. Systemic gendered racism can account for black women's overrepresentation in this field, as domestic work was thought to be the province of women, and blacks were seen as best suited for slavery. This work was extremely exploitative, with black women domestics subject to very low wages, sexual harassment at the hands of white male employers, and high rates of mental, emotional, and sometimes physical abuse.[43] In a society where systemic gendered racism limited most black women's opportunities as paid workers to low-wage jobs like domestic work, entrepreneurship was a more economically lucrative option.

Black female entrepreneurs responded to this systemic gendered racism by engaging in business ownership in a field shaped by these messages. They created and sold products that enabled black women to conform more to the dominant dictates of beauty, which mandated long, straight hair on women.

They also employed other black women in these endeavors, creating a workforce of women who could personally testify to how these products helped them to achieve a sense of beauty denied by systemic gendered racism. As the beauty industry migrated from door-to-door sales to storefronts, these salons became places where black women could, in the company of each other, continue to create a space where they "became beautiful" despite the messages of systemic gendered racism which said otherwise.

Today, the black hair industry still shows signs of being influenced by systemic gendered racism. Contemporary systemic gendered racism still argues that black women, by virtue of being black, are less attractive and feminine than their white counterparts. Although some black women celebrities are now considered great beauties, we should not confuse this with an acceptance of black women, in general, as beautiful. Indeed, systemic gendered racism in the media works to promote the beauty of black women like actress Halle Berry, singer Beyonce Knowles, and model Tyra Banks, who, with their long hair and light skin, still fit Eurocentric rather than Afrocentric beauty norms. Systemic gendered racism still suggests to black women that they are less feminine and attractive, which has implications in social, economic, even occupational spheres.[44] Hair is still a symbol used to reinforce this message of black women's subordinate standing. For some—not all—black women, straightening hair may be a reaction to systemic gendered racism which suggests that black women's hair in its natural state is ugly and unmanageable.[45] Thus, the fact that many black beauty salons count relaxers—the process by which black women's natural hair is chemically straightened—as the cornerstone of their profits may reflect how systemic gendered racism is implicit in the economic success of these salons.

In this chapter, I have attempted to detail how black women's entrepreneurship in the hair industry is best understood in the context of the systemic gendered racism they faced. Next, I turn to modern-day black women who own businesses in the hair industry to explore the impact of systemic gendered racism in shaping their entrepreneurial experiences and creating a racial enclave economy. I posit that black beauty salons are one example of a racial enclave economy, in that they reflect the realities of systemic gendered racism.

CHAPTER THREE

Business Decisions in
the Racial Enclave Economy

"I didn't understand business, until I had one. That was my goal, owning
a business was my goal from the beginning, but then when I got one I realized there was more to it. I got a lot at an early age, but I didn't really
understand it. My employer/employee skills were lacking. But my client-
getting skills were fine, and that's actually what's most important."

—Carrie, 50

Carrie's salon is located in a low-income part of the city that houses several
run-down rowhouses and abandoned buildings. At 50 years old, she is married with two children. Before moving into the hair industry, her only work
history consisted of jobs at several fast-food restaurants. Upon completing
hair school and earning her cosmetology license, Carrie worked as a stylist
only for a short time before transitioning into ownership at the age of 23.
This is the time period she describes in the above quote, when she was
abruptly thrown into entrepreneurship without clearly understanding what
that would entail. Years later, however, Carrie has mastered the things that
she previously did not know about relating to clients and stylists. She inter-
acts comfortably with her stylists and is visibly proud of her salon and the
bustling community of women that it services.

This chapter examines the black beauty salon as an example of a business
in the racial enclave economy. The racial enclave economy is characterized
in part by the existence of entrepreneurial ventures in which the owners react to gendered racism in shaping their business decisions. In this chapter, I

focus on the ways in which this criterion is applicable to black women beauty shop owners. Owners react to gendered racism in making many of their entrepreneurial decisions, including what type of business to open, when to turn to entrepreneurship, as well as the location and financing of the business.

Selecting a Type of Business

As stated in chapter 2, media are an enormously influential proponent of gendered racism. Media images of black women as less feminine, appealing, and attractive than women of other racial groups are rampant, particularly in television and film.[1] These derogatory images have an adverse effect on black women in occupational, social, and even economic spheres.[2] They also influence black women on a personal level, affecting their self-esteem. Research on racial differences in black and white girls' self-esteem suggests that black girls are able to deflect the implication that the narrowly defined beauty images perpetuated in magazines and other media were ideal. Tellingly, however, they remain susceptible to the idea that hair—specifically straight, long hair—is an important marker of beauty.[3] Other research corroborates the idea that media are an extremely effective progenitor of the idea that black women's hair, in its natural state, is something to be corrected or fixed, and that black women must consciously work to resist succumbing to this viewpoint.[4]

Workplaces can also function as agents of gendered racism that present the idea that black women's hair is undesirable and needs to be fixed or altered to look more like white women's hair. In some workplaces, hairstyles that are considered too "ethnic" are restricted. Unsurprisingly, hairstyles like cornrows, dreadlocks, and other hairstyles that are more likely to be worn by blacks are classified as undesirable and therefore restricted. In recent years, Six Flags of America, Marriott Hotels, and the Washington D.C. Fire Department have all received attention for policies that prohibit these hairstyles on their employees.[5]

As such, many black women internalize the idea that "their hair is a problem that must be solved, a territory that must be controlled, above all a part of the black female body that must be fixed."[6] Hair carries social significance and meaning for various groups of women, and for some black women, this significance is manifested in the choice to wear certain hairstyles—afros, braids, dreadlocks—as a symbol of their resistance to racial and gendered beauty norms.[7] Other black women interpret certain hairstyles as a way to improve their appearance, and still others downplay or refuse to attach any social significance to their choices in how to wear their hair. Ultimately, however, hair remains a contested territory for many black women, one that reflects the intersections of race and gender, and one that is subject to the messages of inferiority perpetuated by gendered racism.

Consequently, the desire to "make black women feel beautiful" was cited as the most common reason the black women interviewed for this study went into the hair industry rather than another area. As black women, these owners were subjected to the same social messages about black women's hair as were their customers. They knew firsthand that because of its racial and gendered significance, hair could take on heightened importance for black women. As such, these owners took genuine pleasure in working with black women's hair and spoke frequently of the joy of getting black women to feel beautiful as one of the major factors that initially drew them into this work. Owners "smiled when they spoke of their work [and] talked about the pleasure they took in being able to make someone else look attractive."[8]

Kendra is a salon owner who has been in business for four years. When asked how she became interested in working in the hair industry, she replied:

> I've always had an interest in hair. I always looked at people and said, you know, people with low self-esteem are the real pretty ones. They just don't know it yet, and I just wanted to be the one to bring that out in them. Especially black women, you know hair can be a big thing with us.

Kendra got her start in the hair business by styling hair for her black American friends in junior high school. Seeing how she was able to make these black women feel beautiful, especially in light of societal messages that suggest just the opposite, had a definitive impact on her career goals.

Maxine is another salon owner who has been in business for seven years. She owns a small salon located on the third floor of a walk-up building in an urban part of the city. Maxine describes one of the biggest advantages to her work as the fact that:

> We know black women, we know black hair, and we know what black women want and need for their hair. The majority of our client base is black women and, as black women, we know our clientele well and what they want and like. And I think that is an advantage. One of the nicest things about this work is making other black women feel pretty, that reaction you get from clients. They may come in and their hair's a mess, but I can fix it up, they smile, say thank you, and it looks nice at the end. I like to be able to do that.

Maxine thus underscores the joy she takes as a black woman in helping other black women to feel beautiful. This is especially valuable in a society that, because of systemic gendered racism, often ignores or denies black women's beauty.

Similarly, Lola is 39 and owns a salon in the suburbs of a major city. She is a sole operator and has worked this way for the last six years, although she has ten years of experience in the hair industry. She unequivocally states that:

> The most rewarding part of owning a salon is making black women feel good about themselves. Black women, we think we can do our own hair but you shouldn't. Being a black woman, I know black hair and know how to do black women's hair.

Here, Lola suggests that the knowledge of black women's hair coupled with the appreciation for being able to help black women feel beautiful is an especially important part of salon ownership.

Jamie is also quite explicit in her initial interests in the hair industry and salon work. She says:

> I always wanted to go to school black and work black. I am more comfortable working with blacks in a black situation. I love to cater to us, and I knew I would get to do that in this job. I have a natural talent for hair, so it makes sense to be here where I can, I don't know, just use that talent for black people.

Jamie's definitive interest in working with and being around other blacks made the hair industry seem like a natural choice.

The owners interviewed here clearly understood that appearance, particularly when it comes to hair, holds a certain importance for black women. Thus, making other black women look and feel beautiful became something they greatly enjoyed. The genuine satisfaction they gained from doing this heavily influenced their decisions to pursue full-time work in the hair industry. They were able to create entrepreneurial ventures that were, in part, a reaction to the gendered racism in social spheres. This gendered racism creates a market of black women for whom having hair styled and cared for takes on particular significance reflecting race and gender.

Transitioning to Entrepreneurship

Owners' awareness of the large available market of black women customers—a market influenced by systemic gendered racism—allowed them flexibility in determining when to transition into entrepreneurship. All of the salon owners interviewed here began their work in the hair industry employed as stylists in another salon. They usually worked as stylists anywhere from three to seven years before venturing into self-employment. For many of the women interviewed here, their firsthand knowledge that many black women place high importance upon having their hair professionally styled when transitioning to entrepreneurship affected their decisions about when to move from paid labor to self-employment.

In general, there were two trajectories that described the path these entrepreneurs took from being stylists to owners. Owners in the first trajectory worked as stylists, saved their money carefully, and when they were financially prepared, made the transition to self-employment. Owners in the second trajectory began working as stylists but moved into self-employment rather spontaneously, without much forethought or planning.

The owners who followed the second trajectory are the ones who are especially noteworthy for this research. Their decision to move quickly and impulsively into self-employment was done with a marked lack of fear, worry, or apprehension about maintaining a client base. This was the case for older single women like Lola, who had never been married and had no other sources of income, and with younger married women like Greta, who could rely on her husband's income to support their family through difficult times. More noteworthy, even in the periods when some of these women went into debt, they still did not worry about their long-term success in the field with regards to having a clientele. Their reasons for this specifically reflect entrepreneurial decisions shaped by systemic gendered racism. In short, these women felt that even a quick move into entrepreneurship in the hair industry would pan out for them financially in the end because, as one respondent put it, "Black women love to get their hair done." Owners knew that even if they faced temporary hardships, the available market of black women would eventually assure them a stable client base and, they predicted, economic stability.

Maxine, quoted previously, is an owner who transitioned into entrepreneurship rather hurriedly. She had been working as a stylist for several years when a space opened up for rent two doors away from her place of employment. Since the space was available, she seized the opportunity to rent it and establish her own salon. However, Maxine was not daunted by the prospect of suddenly becoming a business owner. She attributes her lack of fear to her perception that:

> Black women want to get their hair done. At the very beginning when you're starting out it can be rough, but at the point where I went out on my own, I wasn't worried. I had clients and I knew I'd be all right.

Maxine felt that going into business alone would not present problems for her in terms of securing a clientele. This perception stems from owners' awareness of systemic gendered racism, and the understanding of the importance of appearance, particularly in regards to hair, for black women.

Lola echoes Maxine's statements about the reliability of black women as a potential pool for work in this area:

> Customer service is the main thing because people want to get their hair done. Black women will get their hair done. It's not that difficult to own, in that respect. You don't worry about not having business. You'll have business. I will always be in business.

Again, Lola's confidence in moving to self-employment stems in part from what she perceives as the stable market of black women. She asserts that she can and will always remain in business, because "there will always be black women who need to get their hair done."

Donette is another owner who speaks to the constancy of black women as a market for salon owners' services. She describes initially going into business with one stylist who would accommodate white customers, and another who prefers to work primarily with black customers. Donette suggests that while working primarily with black customers closes this stylist off from the market of white customers who may patronize the shop, in the long run this does not hurt this stylist too severely. For one thing, Donette sees few white customers in her salon. Additionally, relying on a predominantly black clientele is not too risky because:

> You know black women, we'll get our hair done. If we do not do anything else, we will go to the salon and get our hair done. So, you know, it's a good thing for stylists. It's a good thing for me as a businesswoman!

Owners in these interviews repeatedly raised this notion of black women as a dependable market. The idea that "black women will get our hair done" was routinely evoked as one of the reasons black women salon owners were so self-assured about moving from paid work to self-employment. They could move into salon ownership without much worry because they felt that the reality of gendered racism essentially assured them a client base and eventual financial stability.

The importance of "getting hair done" is largely rooted in gendered norms that women should be beautiful and attractive, but it is important to underscore the racialized aspects to these gendered norms. The social message that it is incumbent upon women to devote time and energy to hair (and other aspects of beauty) is not racially specific. Indeed, many women of other racial groups may also "love to get their hair done." However, the emphasis on styling hair as a pathway to beauty exists in a racialized context wherein black women's hair is considered a marker of their devalued status and inability to conform to dominant beauty norms. Thus, while women of all racial groups may be subjected to gendered messages that it is important to spend time, energy, and money on their hair, black women receive these messages in a context that simultaneously suggests that their hair requires more work than most to meet acceptable beauty standards.[9]

Finding Financing: Alternatives to Traditional Sources of Start-up Capital

Systemic gendered racism shapes black women salon owners' entrepreneurial decisions about which field to enter and when, in ways that function to their benefit. In other words—like the earlier entrepreneurs Butler describes who are able to market their goods and services to a protected niche untapped by segregation—black women entrepreneurs in the hair industry are able to develop businesses that speak to the needs of other black women who are affected by the systemic gendered racism that disparages and devalues their hair, sense of beauty, and ultimately their femininity.[10] Salon owners' firsthand familiarity with this niche, and their ability to develop businesses that appeal to this niche, embody some of the easier aspects of establishing businesses in the racial enclave economy.

However, gendered racism also created problems for black women salon owners. In some cases, it limited or constrained their business decisions. Systemic gendered racism influenced black women's business decisions in terms of exposing them to a reliable, dependable market and by instilling a desire to meet a need often denied to black women. But it also influenced other business decisions in less advantageous ways.

One business decision that was adversely affected by systemic gendered racism involved the issue of securing start-up funding for the business. All the women interviewed indicated that like most other businesses, launching a hair salon required significant amounts of economic capital. These women had to be prepared to either buy or rent property in which to house the salon. They also had to buy the necessary equipment for the salon—multiple hooded hair dryers, stations to wash hair, mirrors, shampoo, conditioner, and other supplies. Owners also bought furniture to establish a comfortable and relaxed atmosphere in the salon, like sofas, easy chairs, artwork, coffee tables, and televisions. Finally, they had to be financially prepared to cover monthly operating costs, which included electricity, water, and heating bills.

As discussed earlier, the women interviewed for this study all hailed from working-class backgrounds. They were not economically privileged in the sense that they already had economic capital available to pour into their salons. Working as stylists enabled these women to secure greater economic stability than they had been able to procure in their previous jobs. However, when they decided to shift to business ownership, they normally did so with the knowledge that this would require additional amounts of economic capital to which they did not always have immediate access. This meant that owners had to identify ways in which to access the funding needed to launch their salons. They typically identified three possible routes to economic capital: using traditional sources (banks, government funding agencies), capitalizing on social networks (relying on family and friends), or establishing personal savings (carefully saving the money themselves).

None of the women interviewed for this study were able to secure funding for their start-up expenses through traditional sources like banks. This is not to say that they did not make the effort. Many of the women interviewed suggested that despite having business plans, solid credit ratings, and experience in the field, they were denied business loans from banks. They also indicated difficulties accessing funding even through government programs targeted toward minorities interested in entrepreneurship.

Denise is 37 and owns three salons, one of which was passed down to her by her mother. She has been an entrepreneur for six years. The salon in which the interview took place is located in a quiet suburban area. Her other two salons are located in other parts of the city and draw a more working-class clientele. Despite having a family history of entrepreneurship in the hair industry, Denise faced difficulty securing the necessary funds to launch her second salon. She states:

> The government will give money to, seems like, everybody else. But when you go to get money for small businesses, we [she makes a gesture to indicate the two of us, as black women] have to go through a lot. So the hard part was trying to get money from the government. That was the hard part. The easy part was having faith in the Lord's will.

Denise's difficulties with government funding are important given her family history and personal experience with salon ownership. Despite this experience and the financial success of her first salon, she still viewed the process of gaining governmental support for her entrepreneurial venture as more of a hindrance than a help.

Tanisha is another owner who faced difficulty getting funding from traditional sources. At 25, Tanisha is one of the youngest owners in the sample. She suggests that her age played into her difficulties in securing start-up capital from traditional sources:

> At first, it was really hard trying to find out where you're going to get the money from. Because a young person like, I, I'm—you're not thinking to save money for a business. . . . I was working day by day. I didn't have the money. I couldn't get a loan, so . . . I couldn't get grants either, so I had to find money elsewhere.

Tanisha stresses that her early stages of entrepreneurship were by far the most stressful because of the challenges of getting the necessary funding.

Delilah also mentions that when starting out, she had little knowledge of government programs targeted toward minorities:

> The only thing that I didn't know about back then that I do know about now are black businesswomen's loans, things like that. I didn't know about those back then. Um, loans that you can get from certain organizations, government, loans that you can get as a (quote unquote) "underprivileged" person. You know, to open up your own business. I didn't know about those things then. I do know about them now. Although. at this point, it's really not necessary.

Delilah has been a salon owner for fifteen years, so gaining start-up capital is no longer an urgent issue for her. However, her comment further underscores the fact that funding from traditional sources was not a central way in which these owners secured the capital for self-employment.

Studies of other minority entrepreneurs have documented the difficulty of gaining economic capital for entrepreneurship from traditional sources. Racial/ethnic minority men and all women are disproportionately likely to rely on nontraditional sources of funding to secure the necessary start-up capital to switch from paid labor to self-employment.[11] I argue here that the unavailability of funding from government sources and financial institutions reflects the influence of gendered racism in the economic sphere. Rather than attribute the biases within finance centers to race or gender, I suggest that systemic gendered racism helps to construct minority men and minority women as unattractive candidates for loans, as they are routinely denied business and residential loans at higher rates than white counterparts with comparable credit and income.[12] Most of the black women salon owners interviewed here had to combat the gendered racism that they encountered in financial institutions in the form of deprived access to traditional sources of economic capital. Importantly, owners like Denise specifically identified issues of race *and* gender as part of the problem accessing traditional funding sources.

In the absence of government or bank financing, owners were forced to turn to other sources for the necessary start-up capital for their entrepreneurial ventures. Generally, women relied on one of two alternate sources of funding: relying on friends and family or establishing personal savings that they then used to launch the business. As such, the business decision to obtain start-up capital from friends, family, or personal savings illustrates one way that businesses in the racial enclave economy are shaped by gendered racism.

Like Denise, Donette also describes the task of generating start-up capital as an enormous feat, and one of the most difficult aspects of entrepreneurship. Rather than pinning her hopes on funding from banks or government sources, she secured economic capital from friends and family:

> When I wanted to open, my ex-husband, he had several businesses so he just fronted the money and it was really easy. He gave me the money, my business partner at the time got money from her fiancé, and we just went out and bought everything brand new. And we were doing fine.

In Donette's case, relationships with partners (a husband and a fiancé) made the crucial difference in gaining the money to start the business. This underscores how this decision-making process is gendered, in that these women were able to rely on men (who generally are better paid and maintain a higher position in the socioeconomic strata relative to women) for capital. Even among blacks, where women may work more consistently, black men as a group tend to earn higher median incomes. This source of funding may also demonstrate the effects of gendered racism within families, in that black men as significant others were able to offer the requisite economic capital to their ex-wives and fiancées so they could become business owners.

Similarly, Miranda talks about the important role her husband played in generating start-up capital:

> When I first started out, like I said, I was married at the time and we really sacrificed to start out, to open. . . . My husband, he was able to get a loan, so from that one loan he got, that's what we started the business off with. And with that, I was basically able to keep things going.

Like Donette, being married to someone who had or could access economic capital was extremely important in facilitating these women's shift to self-employment.

Not all the owners in this sample were married at the time that they transitioned into salon ownership. Others were married but their husbands did not have access to funds that they could use to offset the costs of establishing a business. These husbands' employment helped to subsidize expenses during the early days of entrepreneurship, but did not offer much assistance in the way of helping to finance the salon. In the absence of other options, these owners simply had to save money from their work as stylists to be able to afford the economic costs of self-employment.

Tanisha is one such owner who had to establish savings that she specifically earmarked for opening her salon. She says:

> It was so hard [to get the money together to open]. I basically had to do it by saving as I worked. What else could I do? As I was working, I had stuff on layaway. But it was hard, it was very hard. Very hard. It didn't happen overnight. I mean, I did most of the stuff when I first opened. But then everything came together.

Tanisha is a single mother of a 6 year old son. Consequently, there is a stark contrast between her difficulties in saving meticulously to open her salon and Donette's assessment that "it was really easy" to get money from her husband.

Denise, the owner who criticized the government for its unwillingness to loan money to black women entrepreneurs, said, "When it came down to it, I had to rely on myself. That's what got us into the other place, across town. Not the government, but I had to depend on myself." Like Tanisha, Denise has never been married. These women are therefore much more likely to emphasize the difficulty of relying on themselves and slowly saving money to cover the initial costs of entrepreneurship.

Unlike Tanisha and Denise, Greta is an owner who was married at the time she decided to transition into salon ownership. However, unlike Donette and Miranda, Greta's husband did not have access to economic capital that she could infuse into her salon. Thus:

> When I decided I wanted open a shop it was three years before I actually did it. I started to save money, buy furniture, supplies, all the stuff I knew I would need. When I relocated to a different area, that was a minor setback, but I just continued to save until I could afford to start my own shop. Since I saved so

much, it turned out to be a good thing that I didn't have a loan because I didn't go into any debt trying to finance the business.

Even though she was married at the time she transitioned into salon owner-ship, Greta's experience generating start-up capital more closely resembles that of the unmarried entrepreneurs in the study.

Again, the difficulties generating economic capital are not themselves unique to black women entrepreneurs. Minority men and other racial mi-nority women face challenges accessing start-up financing for businesses. This aspect of systemic gendered racism does not affect only black women in their efforts toward entrepreneurship.

Challenges of Money Management

Gendered racism also affected salon owners' business decisions when it came to money management. Generally, blacks have less access to financial and investment information than do whites.[13] Many white families also enjoy an intergenerational transfer of wealth as well as the cultural and social capital that facilitates generating more wealth. In contrast, black families are much more likely to start with little or no wealth, and thus transmit less wealth and less knowledge of wealth-producing strategies vertically through generations. These factors contribute to a striking wealth gap wherein black families hold just ten cents of wealth for every dollar held by white families.[14]

No research that I know of has explored how gender may affect racial wealth disparities. In other words, empirical studies have not yet been un-dertaken that examine whether and how the consequences of this institu-tional inequality is gendered. The systemic racism perspective would argue that as whites have economically exploited blacks' labor over the years, whites have consequently been able to bequeath the financial benefits of this exploitation to their children, creating a net white advantage and a black disadvantage in terms of wealth accumulation. However, in taking gender into consideration, we might question whether black women are less likely than black men to have access to wealth given their greater concentration in lower-paying jobs, or if the disproportionate number of black female-headed households in poverty might further constrain intergenerational wealth transfers.[15] Systemic gendered racism may thus have a particular impact on black women or black men that has not been addressed in existing literature on wealth inequality.

For the black women interviewed in this study, systemic gendered racism meant less knowledge about and access to developing wealth. Many owners lamented either their lack of knowledge about producing wealth or the fact that they learned ways to generate wealth relatively late in their careers as entrepreneurs. They shared that salon ownership had brought financial returns in that they were able to count their business as a form of wealth and that they now generated higher incomes (discussed further in the next chapter), but that they had begun to realize that had they known more about investment opportunities, they could have greatly increased their economic rewards. Thus, even owners who, at the time of the interview, were actively involved in wealth producing enterprises like investments and establishing other businesses often regretted that they had only recently learned of these financial opportunities.

Melinda is one owner who speaks to this issue. Though she has only owned her salon for three years, she is beginning to think about the long-term future and what will happen when she retires. She said, "I wish I'd known starting out, if you prepare early for retirement, you can have a lot when you retire. You can invest and have so much money for retirement. No one taught me that coming in." Without that essential knowledge of how and what to invest to prepare adequately for retirement, however, Melinda is forced to recognize that the money she is now putting away for her retirement could have been greatly maximized had she known how to do so.

Miranda offers a similar response. When asked about the hardest part of being a salon owner, she replies:

> Finances, management. I had to learn that, and I'm still learning, to be honest. I'm taking classes now to help with my business skills. I think whatever class that you could get to help with your business is excellent.

Without early knowledge of investment opportunities, Miranda is now taking classes to help her in maximizing the financial returns of her entrepreneurship.

Lana echoes these women's statements when she acknowledges the disparity between what she has earned and what she could have earned: "Probably with the amount of money I made in this industry, the only regret that I have is that I wasn't a better manager of my money . . . working smart is better than working hard, but you learn as you go." As she indicates, the absence of money management knowledge ultimately impaired Lana's potential earnings.

Carrie is 50 and has owned her current salon for nine years. Her shop is adjacent to a poor and somewhat unsafe neighborhood in the eastern part of the city. She says that she will be at her peak as an entrepreneur when "I have other businesses. I want to have other businesses as investments. I'd own homes to rent, things like that that are easy money. I just don't know how to go about doing it exactly, but I'm learning." As these owners learn strategies for investment and for effective money management late in life, their efforts to catch up reflect the systemic racism that helps maintain the wealth gap between blacks and whites.

These owners noticed similar patterns among their stylists as well. Many owners cited a marked lack of money management knowledge among their employees, observing that stylists knew little about ways to channel their income into financial investments that would offer them economic security over the long term. Denise witnesses this among stylists at her salon and among black women in the profession in general:

> A lot of stylists lose out because their money goes right out of their pocket, and at the end of the week they have nothing to show. They have no organization. They put it in the pocket, and spend it out the pocket, so at the end of the week half of them don't even know how much they make. And that's a downfall for a lot of black stylists. They can't grow. This is a problem because it's a way that African American women are not professional in this industry, and it hurts us in the end.

Denise is unequivocal in her belief that the black stylists she observes have very real difficulties maximizing the earnings they make at the salon. Unlike Maxine, Miranda, and Carrie, she does not include herself in this category, but she still observes the manifestations of the lack of money management skills and knowledge among black women in this field.

Tanisha also talks about observing others in the hair industry with lackluster money management skills. However, she focuses on other owners who may not recognize the importance of managing money well: "If owners know how to manage their money, it's a good investment. Because you can get out of hand and don't manage your money right. But everyone don't [sic] know how to do that." Again, the issue of not knowing how to manage money well or to make lucrative financial investments is cited.

Several examples are given of black women's unawareness of how to manage money to gain the most from work in the hair industry. However, as speculated, the consequences of this unawareness are gendered. Specifically, one consequence of black women's constrained knowledge of producing wealth related to the manner in which they supported their families. Several owners expressed the consequences of their lack of money management knowledge in terms of what it meant for their children.

Maxine, for example, specifies her regrets at learning about investment opportunities so late in her career as a salon owner. She said, "I raised my three kids. I'm doing fine. Of course, I'd like to make more—that's one of the things, that's why I wish I'd known more about ways to manage my money earlier. But I'm making a living." In the context of being a mother and raising children, the lack of knowledge Maxine had about money management takes on particular significance. Had she known more about investment opportunities and ways to maximize her income as a salon owner, this knowledge could potentially have been applied to improving her and her children's standard of living.

Similarly, Miranda talks about the how having little information on money management had a particular effect on her family's standard of living:

> If you know to do this—which I didn't—if you can start off investing that investment is excellent. Say if you were to buy a piece of property where it may have an apartment on the upstairs, where if that's bringing money in, you know, you can have your business downstairs and whatever. . . . When I first started out, not knowing that, there were a lot of times we were without things. The children, they were fine, no one knew but us. But those were the hardest times.

Miranda acknowledges that her children were fine, that they never went hungry or lacked other basic necessities. But she also clarifies that during this time, her finances were perhaps at their most insecure, and that this is partly because of how little she knew about investment opportunities that would maximize her income.

Thus, the lack of knowledge of money management options has a particular effect on black women entrepreneurs. Not only do these women demonstrate knowing little about financial opportunities (a finding that reflects the arguments about blacks' constrained access to wealth), but they also concede that this lack of knowledge has implications for their families. Though none of the women suggested that they struggled financially as a result of salon ownership (to be discussed more in chapter 4), they were aware that more knowledge of money management would have meant more to offer their families. Again, this is not to suggest that this aspect of gendered racism only affects black women—certainly other race/gender groups are also limited in their knowledge of money management—but it should draw attention to the ways that systemic gendered racism shapes their particular experiences as entrepreneurs.

Summary

In this chapter, I examine how black women salon owners' business decisions are influenced by gendered racism, thus fulfilling one characteristic of businesses in the racial enclave economy. In the process of becoming entrepreneurs, black women salon owners faced several important decisions: what type of business to open, when to move from paid work to self-employment, how to gain access to start-up capital, and how to invest the economic capital the salon generated. The choices these women made when faced with these decisions reflected the influence of gendered racism. The broader social messages that black women are unattractive and unfeminine are aspects of gendered racism that are implicated in black women's decisions to pursue entrepreneurship in the hair industry and mitigate many concerns about timing the transition from paid work to self-employment. Gendered racism also impacts the ways black women entrepreneurs attempt to access start-up funding; it also affects their lack of knowledge of investment opportunities. The impact of gendered racism on these business decisions exemplifies how these beauty salons can be considered as examples of businesses in the racial enclave economy.

The gendered racism that shapes these women's business decisions is systemic and experienced through economic institutions and social spheres. Gendered racist ideologies and images that depict black women as unattractive, unfeminine, and socially devalued are systemic and widespread. Workplaces reinforce this message when they prohibit hairstyles like dreadlocks and cornrows that are popular among blacks with natural, unprocessed hair. Requirements like this contribute to the image of black women—and their hair—as inherently unattractive, and reinforce the widespread idea that black women must work harder to be considered feminine and beautiful.[16] Media further perpetuate the idea that black women are less attractive than other women. Ultimately, this gendered racist idea of black women as devalued and unfeminine is systemic and becomes something black women encounter in a variety of public spaces, institutions, and social settings.

Given the systemic and widespread nature of gendered racism, when owners like Kendra, Maxine, and Lola describe their sense of personal gain and their feeling that they are contributing to a greater social good, they also describe reasons for choosing entrepreneurship in the hair industry that have particular significance. These owners are motivated to do this work in order to counter the systemic, gendered racist images of black women that abound in society. Because they are black women who are also subjected to and experience this systemic gendered racism, they know firsthand what messages black women are encountering. This knowledge intimately shapes their business decisions when considering what type of entrepreneurial venture to pursue and when to transition into ownership.

As gendered racism is systemic, it is perpetuated not only in social settings and in the workplace, but also through economic institutions. Lending institutions' documented failures in offering financial support to women and racial minorities is yet another indication of the systemic nature of gendered racism. Black women's limited knowledge of money management also has gendered, racialized consequences. Thus, black women's constrained access to funding and financial investment options represents one of the ways their business decisions reflect the systemic, pervasive impact of gendered racism.

CHAPTER FOUR

A Pathway to Financial Security

This is really a field where black women can do well . . . and it's important to me that people understand that and respect this industry.

—Lana, 44

Lana is passionate about the hair industry and her work within it. When I arrived at her salon to interview her, she was blow-drying a customer's hair and carrying on simultaneous conversations with that customer and another stylist. When we adjourned to the basement of her salon for her interview, she described having worked in the hair industry since her late teens. This business, she told me, was all she wanted to do and all she knew how to do. She was very proud of her accomplishments as a salon owner, and felt that it was her mission to combat the disrespect that she saw as endemic to jobs in the service industry. She felt that pushing stylists to take a more professional approach to their jobs would get people to offer the respect that she felt work in the hair industry truly deserved. For Lana, being a salon owner was not simply a job, it was crucial to her identity and her standing in the community.

Lana is correct in her assessment that workers in the service industry are often treated disrespectfully.[1] Black women in particular are frequently channeled into low-paying, undesirable positions in the service and other industries. In this chapter, I argue that gendered racism in the labor market plays a role in constraining black women in these limiting jobs. Entrepreneurship thus becomes an attractive option that offers greater financial security than paid work in a labor market shaped by gendered racism. When black workers turn to entrepreneurship because of the systemic gendered racism that permeates the labor market, their entrepreneurship becomes part of a racial enclave economy.

This aspect of the racial enclave economy is similar to the theory of labor market disadvantage. As a theoretical concept, labor market disadvantage purports to explain entrepreneurship by arguing that groups who experience difficulties, challenges, and obstacles in the labor market turn to entrepreneurship as an alternative. Researchers have attempted to apply this theory to blacks, acknowledging that they face severe labor market disadvantage in the form of racial discrimination. However, blacks are often cited as a challenge to this theory, inasmuch as other groups who face less extensive and long-term labor market disadvantage have higher rates of entrepreneurship.[2]

The model of the racial enclave economy offers a more precise explanation for groups' entrepreneurship than the theory of labor market disadvantage. Rather than lumping in racial discrimination with other forms of disadvantage that various groups may experience in the labor market, this theory emphasizes the particular role of racial discrimination—specifically, systemic gendered racism—as one of several important factors that constitute a racial enclave economy. This model thus focuses less on attempting to explain the discrepancy between the extent of disadvantage and the (relatively) low numbers of black entrepreneurs. Rather, it suggests that disadvantage, broadly defined, does not sufficiently explain entrepreneurship, but that systemic gendered racism may be a more compelling explanation.

In this chapter, I explore how systemic gendered racism restricts black women's occupational options, thus exacerbating their difficulties ensuring financial stability. I argue that these constrained options and the limited economic security they provide ultimately facilitate entrepreneurship in the racial enclave economy. Further, I demonstrate how salon ownership enables black women to establish economic security.

A Contemporary Picture of Working-Class
Black Women in the Labor Market

Denigrating the black poor and working class has long been a theme of certain elites, and the last few years have seen a resurgence of themes of self-help and responsibility that blame the black poor, underclass, and working class for their class position. Most notably, entertainer Bill Cosby has scathingly criticized the black underclass for squandering the gains of the Civil Rights movement. Cosby urges black lower-class, working-class, and underclass members to "stop blaming the white man" and to embrace values of hard work and responsibility as a pathway to economic improvement.[3]

Though Cosby's comments have garnered a great deal of media attention and support from conservative pundits, the challenges and difficulties faced by black working-class women are considerably more complex than Cosby indicates.[4] Simply accepting the mandate to work hard does little to challenge the constraints working-class black women face in the labor market. In the labor market, working-class black women face daunting obstacles including racially and gender-specific stereotypes and controlling images, a rapidly shifting economy, substandard schools, dwindling job opportunities, and institutional and individual discrimination from employers.[5] The end result is their overrepresentation in low-paying, low-status jobs.

Working-class black women are generally concentrated in industrial and clerical fields, in low-paying jobs that do not offer benefits.[6] They are often found working as laundry workers, health aides, and cooks—jobs that rarely provide a livable wage for families. When these women are forced to raise families on these salaries, they often require financial assistance from the government and become stereotyped as "welfare queens" and depicted in the media as drains on society.[7] A similar version of the welfare queen stereotype takes form in the image of black women as unreliable single mothers.[8] This stereotype clouds employers' judgments and makes them reluctant to hire black women as employees. Finally, controlling images of working-class black women as "bitches" and "Bad Black mothers" or "welfare mothers" serve to justify the structural constraints that relegate these women to inferior placement in the labor market: "these interconnected representations offer a plausible explanation for poor and/or working-class African American women's class status."[9] Though most of these stereotypes involve characterizations of working-class black women as lazy, poor, and unwilling to work, very little empirical evidence exists to support the claim that working-class black women prefer unemployment and/or financial support from government sources as opposed to paid labor.[10]

Much attention has been given to black women's recent gains and advances in the educational and occupational arenas, with many researchers noting that more black women than men are enrolled in four-year colleges, and that black women are rapidly breaking down barriers in the corporate and political spheres.[11] Like the arguments that blame the black working and underclass for their position, these data are often produced to bolster the claim that institutional barriers have disappeared for blacks. It is true that as a group, black women have experienced unprecedented occupational advancement in the last half-century. Gains from the Civil Rights movement resulted in a shift from black women's overrepresentation in domestic service to their entry into management, corporate, and white-collar work.[12] While this achievement is certainly important and noteworthy, these gains are more commonly seen among middle-class black women and are not necessarily as widespread among their working-class counterparts.

Finally, the economic returns for black women are still not equivalent to their counterparts. Table 4.1 demonstrates that across time, black women's median earnings have never been equal to the median earnings of whites, male and female, or those of black men. Though the gap between median earnings of black men and women has narrowed in the last thirty years, a sizable difference remains. The disparity between black and white women has remained fairly constant, and white males' median earnings continue to far outpace black women's.

Ultimately, working-class black women encounter discrimination, disadvantageous stereotypes, and limited access to important educational opportunities. As a group, they still experience wage disparity with men and white women. Thus, their occupational opportunities are narrowly restricted and rarely afford them economic stability.

Table 4.1.   Median Incomes by Race and Gender

		Male		Female	
		Current $	2005 $	Current $	2005 $
White	2005	35,345	35,345	19,451	19,451
	1995	25,481	32,413	12,807	16,291
	1985	17,692	30,614	7,438	12,871
	1975	9,514	30,426	3,616	11,564
	1965	5,290	27,748	1,613	8,461
Black	2005	22,653	22,653	17,631	17,631
	1995	16,006	20,360	10,961	13,943
	1985	10,768	18,633	6,277	10,862
	1975	5,560	17,781	3,107	9,936
	1965	2,847	14,934	1,174	6,158
Asian American	2005	34,215	34,215	21,641	21,641
	1995	22,162	28,191	12,862	16,361
Latino/a	2005	22,089	22,089	15,036	15,036
	1995	14,840	18,877	8,928	11,357
	1985	11,434	19,785	6,020	10,417
	1975	6,777	21,673	3,202	10,240

Source: www.census.gov/hhes/www/income/histinc/p02.htm/

Work History Prior to Salon Ownership

The work histories of the women interviewed for this study supported the existing research that suggests that working-class black women are usually confined to some of the least desirable jobs. These women described work histories that included low-paying, low-status jobs in the food and personal service industries. In general, these women encountered difficulty establishing financial security and found these jobs personally unfulfilling and unrewarding.

Carrie is a salon owner who is quoted about the beginning of chapter 3. Her work prior to entering the hair industry consisted primarily of jobs in the food service industry. Carrie was employed at several fast-food restaurants before transitioning to the beauty industry. She stated that after high school:

> I worked at Burger King and McDonald's. It did not take long to realize that that was not going to work [laughs]. I went straight to hair school, started working at [names salon], and had my own shop in three years.

Carrie described a rapid ascension from paid employment in the food service industry to entrepreneurship.

Several other owners got their start working in retail prior to moving into the hair industry. Like Carrie, they described their jobs in the retail industry in less than glowing terms. Kendra said, "I've done retail, I used to live in New York where I worked for Bloomingdale's department store. I just did that for a couple years. That was my boring job." Later, Kendra went on to do telemarketing work for several companies. "I worked for Chase Manhattan, actually just doing like telemarketing work. Also Southern Fuel Company; that sounds interesting [said sarcastically]." Similarly, Sarah, an owner who has had her shop for three years, worked at Lowe's prior to deciding to enter the hair industry.

Interestingly, one of the most common fields these owners described as part of their work history prior to moving to the beauty industry involved work in the medical industry. Maxine stated:

> I worked in the billing department at Sacred Heart Hospital for five years. Then I had a baby, and after a few more years I went to another hospital and worked there for two years doing billing work. I had done this before; I did billing and data entry for an oil company, but I always hated it. My passion was doing hair.

Maxine described her work in billing and data entry in an unenthusiastic manner. In contrast to her entrepreneurship as a salon owner, billing and data entry was clearly not work she enjoyed.

Denise is another salon owner whose work history includes employment in the medical field. Although her mother owned a salon, which she passed on to Denise upon retirement, Denise began working "at County General Hospital, in dietary. My mother started this, actually. I worked at two hospitals, one in Alabama and one at County General." Though she had experience working in the medical industry, Denise returned to her mother's salon as an apprentice and quickly climbed the ranks to manager and then owner.

Donette also described a work history that includes the medical industry. Before becoming a salon owner, she "worked in administration at a hospital. I also had worked at a drug rehabilitation center for adolescents." Donette left these jobs after a few years to begin beauty school, and has been working in the hair industry ever since.

Finally, some owners simply avoided paid employment in other sectors of the labor market altogether. They went straight into paid work as stylists, frequently in salons owned by other black women. Greta is one such example of this occupational trend:

> I grew up around this profession. My aunt and my cousin owned salons. My mom and my two other cousins were stylists, so I grew up around this. The only other thing I thought about doing was, after high school, I was going to go to nursing school. But I dropped it, went to beauty school, and I never looked back.

Though Greta ultimately eschewed paid work in another field of the labor market for work in the hair industry, her story maintains some similarity to Maxine, Denise, and Donette in that Greta also considered work in the medical field to be one of few other feasible occupational options.

Miranda also chose to go straight into the hair industry rather than seeking employment elsewhere. After graduating from high school, Miranda:

> took trade up at Dudley's. I took my test there, you take your test and then you do a workshop, and I started working at a shop and was also doing hair in my mother's home. I stayed with this for a little while, and after that, I would say in 1990, I opened up my first shop.

Miranda also reveals a relatively short period of time in paid work before moving on to salon ownership.

The work histories of the salon owners interviewed here reflect the influence of systemic gendered racism on black women's opportunities in the labor force. The jobs these women held prior to transitioning to the hair industry—retail, fast-food workers, billing and data entry technicians, tele-marketing—are typical of the low-paying, low-status, low-prestige positions commonly held by working-class black women. Despite the fact that several women held jobs in the medical field, the types of work in which these women were employed are the jobs with the least prestige, economic reward, and stability. They were not employed in the medical field as doctors or administrators (occupations which are predominantly filled with white men), nor were they employed as nurses (an occupation which is predominantly filled white women). Rather, these women worked in the bottom sector of the medical field, in jobs in which black women are likely to be concentrated.[13]

It is also important to note that these women rarely cited the jobs they held outside the hair industry as ones that allowed them to meet their financial responsibilities to their families. Women generally left their work in other fields to enter the hair industry for two reasons: they felt this work was their calling and they were also well aware of the financial rewards the hair industry offered relative to other jobs they had or had held in the past. Significantly, their financial obligations stemmed largely from familial needs. In other words, these women's work histories prior to entering the hair industry can be characterized as low-paying, unrewarding work that, most importantly, did not offer them the necessary financial stability to provide for their families. In contrast, these women felt that work in the hair industry—and salon ownership in particular—could provide both personal gain and economic stability necessary to care for children.

Charlene gives a particularly to-the-point example of this. Prior to entering the hair industry, she worked as a security guard. When asked why she made the transition from this work to the hair industry, she stated, "I had three kids. I knew I didn't want to be on welfare, and I knew I had to raise my kids. So I went to beauty school." Charlene is quite clear that unlike her work as a security guard, work in the hair industry offered her the financial security she needed to provide for her family's needs.

Other owners cite the economic responsibilities incurred by children or families as reasons for making the move to entrepreneurship. Sarah stated:

> I have a baby, and at Supercuts you have to split like 50 percent with them, and then they take out for the shampoo, they take out for the conditioner. So, I said, I'm not going to keep working for them because I was barely making $500 every two weeks. Being here I can make $500 in a day, or in two days, and it's mine. That, plus I have a baby that I have to take care of, it just made sense.

Sarah's statement is particularly important as it emphasizes the unique challenges faced by working-class black women. For Sarah, the deduction of costs for shampoo and conditioner made work at this chain salon an impractical means for supporting her family. Additionally, given the existence of systemic gendered racism, her other work opportunities were limited.

Other owners discussed noneconomic familial responsibilities as motivators for self-employment in the hair industry. For instance, Donette stated:

> When my son was two he was a cancer patient, and I was working for the city of New York at the time and I couldn't be home with him. Doing hair from home allowed me to generate an income, do hair, and still be with him.

Though Donette did not explicitly cite financial reasons as the impetus for her move to the hair industry, her statement underscored some of the appeal work in the hair industry held for working-class black women. Unlike her job working for the city, work in the hair industry offered Donette the financial stability she needed, as well as the free time and opportunity to care for her young child.

For black women, systemic gendered racism plays a role in the occupational opportunities they encounter in the labor market. Gendered racism limited these working-class black women's work options to low-level work in the medical, food service, or retail industries—undesirable jobs that did not provide sufficient economic return. With the added responsibility of caring for families, existing work options as paid laborers became increasingly insufficient in meeting economic needs. Systemic gendered racism thus shapes these women's opportunities in the paid labor market by restricting them to such low-wage work that entrepreneurship becomes a more attractive option. Salon ownership takes place in response to the ways gendered racism limits these women's other options in the labor market, and thus becomes an example of entrepreneurship in the racial enclave economy.

Economic Stability in the Racial Enclave Economy

Though the women interviewed here transition to entrepreneurship in part because it offers better economic returns than paid work in the general labor market, it is worth addressing exactly whether and how salon ownership facilitates these women's economic improvement. Women generally moved into the hair industry under the perception that they could generate more financial returns in this field. Similarly, they made the transition from paid work to entrepreneurship with the belief that this too was more cost-effective and a better financial investment. The women expected that moving to entrepreneurship offered greater economic stability than paid work in the general labor market and paid work as stylists in the racial enclave economy. This section examines the ways in which salon ownership offered women the opportunities to increase their economic stability.

For the majority of women observed for this research, salon ownership did appear to have a direct impact on their personal incomes, increasing incomes above what they had previously been able to earn as workers inside and outside the hair industry. The women interviewed reported earning revenues from salon ownership that ranged from $35,000 to $100,000 annually. Owners usually subtracted a certain amount from this revenue to pay business-related expenses such as rent and utility and telephone bills. Their personal incomes are the annual salary that they take home after business expenses have been paid. Here, I focus on the changes in the women's personal incomes and wealth acquisition.

While the majority of the women interviewed described increased incomes as a result of salon ownership, women's pathways to increased incomes generally followed one of two trajectories (see table 4.2). Regardless of which trajectory they followed, salon ownership generally enabled these women to increase their incomes and wealth.

Trajectory A
Of the twenty-three women interviewed for this study, eleven followed Trajectory A. Trajectory A is defined partly by women who experience a decline

Table 4.2.   Salon Owners' Trajectories of Socioeconomic Advancement

	Phase I Work outside hair industry	Phase II Work within hair industry	Phase III Opening salon	Phase IV 1-5 years	Phase V 5+ years
Trajectory A	Low but stable incomes, little wealth	Incomes steadily increase	Decline in income, increase in wealth	Income increases, wealth increases	Income and wealth from the salon plateau
Trajectory B	Low but stable incomes, little wealth	Incomes increase some	Income remains stable, increase in wealth	Income and wealth increase	Income and wealth from the salon plateau

upon transitioning to salon ownership (Phase III). In Phase I, when they worked outside the hair industry, they usually earned salaries of around $25,000 annually. During this phase, women rarely owned any wealth other than perhaps a car. Most did not own homes or have other forms of wealth like investments or stocks.

When women began to work in the hair industry, they moved into Phase II. While some of the women left low-paying occupations to move into the hair industry, it is also important to note that not all women once held jobs outside the hair industry. Miranda and Lola went directly into the hair industry to work as stylists and therefore began at Phase II. Upon entering the hair industry, most of the women interviewed worked in salons owned by other African American women. In this phase, the women were able to increase their incomes from what they earned in Phase I.

During Phase III, the women moved from working as stylists to opening their own salons. At this point, these women experienced a decline in income. The decline in income stems from the funds the women must expend in order to open the shop. Expenses associated with opening the business include paying a security deposit to rent a space and the first month's rent, buying furniture, installing shampoo bowls and other necessities, and paying electric and water bills. These expenses can drain funds and force the women to take home less personal income. Accordingly, many owners cited the initial months of opening the shop as the most difficult aspect of entrepreneurship. Some went into debt as a result of trying to finance their shops but most women indicated that the proceeds from their salons enable them to erase their debt within two to three years. Miranda, for example, has been in the hair industry for sixteen years and has been a salon owner for twelve. She talked about how her income declined when she first moved from being a stylist to an owner:

> When I first started out . . . we really sacrificed to start out, to open. There was a lot of times we were without things . . . financially, you just really have to save.

While income declines, Phase III is also the period where women initially began to increase their wealth. As business owners, the women acquired additional wealth in the form of the salon.

Phase IV began when the women's incomes begin to improve. At this point, owners had been in business for at least six months and have hired employees. With stylists in their employ, owners were able to collect booth rent, which leads to a rise in income. In addition, the rise in income led to an increase in wealth. Owners started to accrue wealth in the form of houses, cars, and sometimes investment or stocks. By Phase IV, owners have amassed more wealth and have much higher incomes than they held at Phase I. Tanisha, for example, worked at TJ Maxx as a sales associate until she went to work as a stylist. She opened her salon two years ago. As an owner, Tanisha's personal income exceeds $100,000, which is significantly more than she earned working at TJ Maxx and more than she earned as a stylist.

The women moved into Phase V when the income and wealth they were able to generate from the salon began to stabilize and plateau. By Phase V, the women's incomes had stopped rising and they had a solid clientele and a set number of stylists who contributed a steady monthly amount in booth rent. During Phase V, some women turned to other outlets in order to continue generating wealth. Rather than continuing to invest in homes and cars, the women invested in their businesses in order to increase their wealth. Specifically, they developed their businesses further or opened other salons.

Most salons offered personal services to clients—specifically, straightening, washing, cutting, styling, and/or coloring hair. When trying to further develop their businesses, many salon owners also sold beauty aids products, which enabled them to enhance their monetary intake. In addition to (or in place of) beauty aids products, other owners sold jewelry, clothing, and accessories. Miranda is an owner who is at the beginning of Phase V. Her plans for her salon include opening a boutique on one floor and devoting the other floor to the salon:

> In the short term, I want to have more of the area free so [clients] can shop. Because they love shopping in a boutique. . . . My next [goal] would be being able to really turn this property into a whole "boutique-upstairs, salon-downstairs" type of place. [To] basically turn this whole property into a boutique/salon, or a spa.

Donette is at Phase V as well, and also plans to further develop her wealth by investing in her business. She plans to move south to open another salon but intends to maintain ownership of her current shop.

Trajectory B
The remaining twelve owners' paths to socioeconomic advancement followed Trajectory B. With the exception of Phases II and III, Trajectory B is essentially the same as Trajectory A. Along Trajectory B, women begin in either Phase I or II. Women who began in Phase I worked outside the hair industry in low-wage work. By Phase II, the women entered the hair industry

to work as stylists. However, unlike the women in Trajectory A, during Phase II these women began to save meticulously in order to afford to open their salons. For these women, Phase II involved a rise in income, but the women were very careful to monitor their expenses in preparation for Phase III.

As a result of careful financial planning, when these women entered Phase III they did not experience a decline in income. Instead, their incomes remained stable. Having saved enough to pay for the costs of opening the salon, these women relied on the clientele they established as stylists in order to keep their incomes stabilized. They were also able to increase their wealth at Phase III because they considered the salon as an asset.

By Phase IV, these women, like their counterparts in Trajectory A, began to see increases to income. It is at this point that they hired stylists and were able to collect booth rent, which led to a rise in income. They also began to invest wealth into homes and cars. Greta is one owner who, while working as a stylist, saved meticulously for three years in order to launch her salon in a debt-free manner. After saving so carefully to avoid going into debt during Phase III, Greta currently employs two stylists and earns $60,000 in personal income each year. The booth rent she collects from her two stylists affords her a higher income than what she earned when employed as a stylist. In addition, she has greater wealth than she did as a stylist because she can consider her business as an asset.

During Phase V, the women's incomes stopped increasing and leveled out to consistent, steady revenue. Like the women of Trajectory A, at this point the women began to consider other ways to amass more wealth, usually by further developing their salons. By now, the women no longer sought to invest their wealth only into their cars and houses.

Comparison of Trajectories

The most common factor that differentiated women in Trajectory A from those in Trajectory B had to do with their experiences in the salon where they worked immediately prior to becoming owners. Women who followed Trajectory A were more likely to state that they were not completely satisfied with their place of employment prior to becoming owners. Maxine, Chandra, and Lola had complaints about the shops where they worked as stylists; this played a role in their rapid transition to entrepreneurship. While working as stylists, these women had passing thoughts about becoming owners but found themselves suddenly thrust into ownership when they learned about good deals on available property. After moving quickly to secure the space, these women then realized that they did not have all the money for the other expenditures of salon ownership. They experienced a dip in personal income as heightened business expenses forced them to take home less money in personal income. This experience forced Maxine to follow Trajectory A:

> I hadn't even planned to open a shop at that point. It was something I'd always thought about but I hadn't really prepared for it enough. But the space where I used to work wasn't what I wanted—they just had too many problems, with the plumbing, one time the water line broke. . . . Suddenly this space became available, so I just took advantage of a good opportunity.

Fortunately, by Phases IV and V the women were able to increase their personal incomes as their new businesses stabilized. Maxine is currently earning $50,000 per year and owns her home and a car.

Women who followed Trajectory B were not rushed into salon ownership. They waited to move into entrepreneurship until they were financially prepared for the responsibility. As such, they avoided situations like those faced by the women in Trajectory A, who experienced a difficult period of questioning whether they would be able to keep their salons open and operating. When Delilah was a stylist, she spent four years putting money aside in order to open her salon. She stated, "People always want to rush to get a salon. It's not something you should rush into. It can be very rewarding if you manage your money right, but you have to know how to do that." For Delilah, smart money management meant waiting to establish her shop until she could do so without undergoing any financial setbacks.

Socioeconomic Advancement within the Racial Enclave Economy

Salon ownership allowed these women to experience socioeconomic advancement with regards to income and wealth. They began in what could be considered working-class or working poor backgrounds. None of the women interviewed from this study, prior to entering the hair industry, earned middle- or upper-middle-class incomes, owned assets, investments, or had high levels of educational attainment. Furthermore, none of these women were part of families where the combined household incomes reached the middle-class or upper-middle-class levels. In fact, married women in this study indicated that they were the breadwinners. Salon ownership, therefore, is largely a means by which working-class women can secure middle-class and upper-middle-class incomes and acquire wealth. In this case, self-employment in the racial enclave economy facilitates economic mobility.

For example, Carrie worked at a succession of fast-food jobs before entering the hair industry. She did not own a car, or her home, and did not have enough income with which to procure any other forms of wealth. As a salon owner, she followed Trajectory A and at Phase V, she currently earns $50,000 per year. Carrie also owns her home, a late model Jeep Grand Cherokee, and plans to lease apartments as a path to additional wealth.

Miranda is 36, married, with two children. She has always worked in the hair industry. She began working at a salon immediately after high school, worked as a stylist for four years, and has been an owner for the last twelve. Though she entered the hair industry at Phase II, salon ownership has allowed her to increase her income and her wealth from what she was able to amass as a stylist. During Phase II, Miranda earned $45,000 per year. She owned a car but did not own her home and had no investments. Miranda is now in Phase V. As a salon owner, she was able to buy her home and the property she uses as her salon. Miranda also intends to develop her salon to increase its value as an asset. She also has been able to increase her income to $65,000 per year.

Whether they followed Trajectory A or B, by Phase V the women were all earning higher incomes than they were in Phase I or II. By Phase V, the majority of owners made around $45,000 annually, and three owners indicated that their annual incomes exceeded $85,000 per year. This is in stark contrast to research that contends that small black businesses like the hair salon are declining, low-return investments which leave owners barely subsisting.[14] The data from this study challenge conclusions that small black businesses produce a paltry, irrelevant income for black entrepreneurs, as salon ownership generally enabled black women to increase their incomes to the middle-class bracket and thus to enjoy socioeconomic advancement.

Education and Socioeconomic Advancement

Salon ownership led to socioeconomic advancement with regards to income and wealth but did not lead to socioeconomic advancement in terms of educational attainment. All of the owners had completed high school prior to opening salons. However, salon ownership did not compel the women to pursue any additional education. Of all the owners interviewed, four—Lana, Lola, Clarice, and Denise—had completed two years of college but none of the owners had obtained a college degree or any advanced degrees. In fact, several women stated that after graduating from high school, they simply were not interested in pursuing a college education. When Miranda finished high school, she began working in a salon immediately after graduation. She has owned her own salon for twelve years, and stated:

> When I had to pick out my trade in high school, I took up cosmetology. I didn't, I didn't really want to go to college. I didn't have anything against it. You know how you just go to school, go to school, you kind of get a little tired, and you kind of feel a little off. And if you don't go to college, you know you have to do something with your life. So my mother, she said, "as long as you do something . . ."

Miranda did not display any regret about not attending college and had no plans to pursue further education.

Owning a salon may in fact work to dissuade women from striving for educational attainment. For many owners who completed high school and were able to earn middle- and upper-middle-class salaries from their work at the salon and were also able to acquire wealth, the added expense and time of continuing education did not seem to be essential or worthwhile. Owners were much more likely to continue to obtain further training and education in cosmetology (that is, to learn of new and useful hair products and other trade skills) than to pursue a college education. It may be that owners perceived that cosmetology courses were much more useful to developing their business than a nonvocational college education. Consequently, salon ownership appeared to retard socioeconomic advancement in certain ways.

Socioeconomic Advancement and Class Mobility

Overall, salon ownership for these African American women appeared to lead to improvements in income and wealth, but not to improvements in educational status. Additionally, increases in wealth and income seemed to enable the women to experience upward mobility into the middle or upper-middle classes. Before working in the hair industry, most of the women held working-class jobs with low potential for socioeconomic advancement. As "high school educated operatives, clerical workers, retail sales clerks . . . with family incomes of about $25,000," they would easily be described as working-class.[15] As a result of owning a salon, however, a number of these women were able to transcend their working-class status to enjoy socioeconomic mobility and eventually to attain aspects of the middle- and upper-middle-class lifestyle.

Summary

As a consequence of gendered racism in the labor market, working-class black women find their occupational options limited to jobs that do not pay well enough to offer economic stability. When the added responsibility of raising families is also considered, these women's financial position becomes that much more precarious. The constraints that gendered racism places on these women's occupational options lead them to consider the hair industry as a viable—and more economically lucrative—alternative. Generally, these women are correct in their assessments that work in the hair industry is a pathway to greater financial stability. Salon ownership does enable these women to ascend from the working to the middle class via increased salaries and wealth acquisition, though not through educational attainment. Though generally self-employed women in nonprofessional arenas do not generate the same economic returns as men, rejecting paid employment for salon ownership in the racial enclave economy allowed these women to increase their financial stability.[16]

Again, the challenges these women face in the labor market underscore the systemic nature of gendered racism. In chapter 3, I discussed how systemic gendered racism is perpetuated through the media and economic institutions, shaping these women's business decisions and thus creating a racial enclave economy. This chapter indicates that gendered racism is part of the economic sphere as well, shaping the labor market and black women's opportunities as paid workers. This gendered racism channels black women into low-paying jobs that offer minimal financial security. Entrepreneurship becomes an attractive alternative to the gendered racism of the labor market and the low-level jobs that await black women—particularly black women from working-class backgrounds. As a systemic issue, gendered racism is present not only in social spheres and economic institutions but also in the labor market, depressing black women's job options and opportunities for financial security. However, gendered racism in these areas helps to render entrepreneurship a tempting option.

The systemic nature of gendered racism does not push only working-class black women toward entrepreneurship. In the introduction to this book, I noted that professional black women also describe owning their own business as a way to escape from racist, sexist corporate cultures. For working-class black women, gendered racism in the labor market limits their occupational options and makes entrepreneurship desirable; for black professional women, experiences with gendered racism in the corporate workplace push them toward entrepreneurship. That both groups of women are responding to gendered racism in different spheres underscores its widespread, systemic nature and far-reaching impact.

CHAPTER FIVE

Stereotypes and Social Support

Some women will really get into trouble because their shop is, I hate to say this, but it's ghetto. And their shops are ghetto because they're ghetto. That only attracts a certain type of business.

—Clarice, 43

You can do the same thing that I do. If you need help, I'll help you. I don't mind.

—Tanisha, 25

Clarice was one of the few respondents in this study who had attended college. She realized during her sophomore year at the state university that what she really wanted to do was work full time in the hair industry, and concluded that she was therefore wasting her time—and her mother's money—by remaining in school. She went to cosmetology school and has since alternated between being a sole operator with no employees and having small shops with very few stylists. Like most of the owners interviewed here, she had several friends and acquaintances in the hair industry. Moreover, like the other owners who spoke about the industry in general and the women who comprised it, Clarice identified certain populations less than favorably.

Entrepreneurial venues in the racial enclave economy develop in response to the systemic gendered racism that owners experience in the larger society. Owners' experiences with gendered racism in the labor market push them toward business ownership, as they conceptualize entrepreneurship as a more viable work option that offers greater possibilities for economic security and in many cases, economic mobility. Gendered racism also informs their decisions as entrepreneurs, shaping when to go into business and which types of businesses they will establish.

In many ways, black women have been able to turn the disadvantages of systemic gendered racism into economically lucrative business endeavors. They respond to the constraints of gendered racism in the labor market by establishing their own businesses. They address the gendered racism in the media and in the workplace that renders black women's hair unmanageable and unattractive, and develop businesses to target this particular market. Consequently, in many ways the black beauty salon functions as a site that defies the messages of black women's devaluation, which are inherent in systemic gendered racism. However, even as black salon owners construct the salon as a social space that challenges systemic gendered racism, in many ways these challenges embody contradictions and paradoxes. Thus, the black beauty salon both defies and reifies the gendered racism that exists in larger society.

The previous chapters explore how gendered racism in economic institutions, media, social arenas, and the labor market structures black women's entrepreneurial work by creating external pressures that facilitate their transition to business ownership. This chapter explores how gendered racism plays a role in the daily interactions in the salon on a micro level. Specifically, this chapter explores the ways in which black women's interactions at the salon simultaneously serve to replicate and challenge the gendered racism of the larger society.

Challenging Systemic Gendered Racism: The Helping Ideology

Systemic gendered racism is embedded in various institutions in American society, and serves to promote particular societal messages about various groups. Ideologies of systemic gendered racism generally foster an environment of mistrust, suspicion, and devaluation of black women.[1] In particular, gendered racist ideology encourages competition between black women in numerous arenas—the workplace, for men, or for other social rewards.

In the workplace, especially in professional work settings, black women encounter frequent challenges that impede their occupational advancement—concrete ceilings, discrimination, difficulty securing mentorship, exclusion from necessary social networks.[2] Consequently, the perception often arises that there is room for very few black women "at the top."[3] With the idea that very few, if any, black women will ascend to coveted heights within professional organizations, black women may be motivated to compete with other black women for choice positions, promotions, and other occupational rewards. Working-class black women also face challenges in the workplace, including the pressure of adapting to new social norms, values, and cultures of certain work environments and difficulty finding mentors who could model a path to upward mobility.[4]

Researchers have documented the emergence of a similar paradigm in heterosexual relationships among black Americans. Numerous aspects of systemic gendered racism have served to reduce the available pool of "marriageable black men."[5] The decline in manufacturing jobs and skilled labor, coupled with constantly decreasing funding for schools has rendered record numbers of black men unable to find steady, consistent employment that offers a living wage. As sociopolitical and legal changes mandate heavy punishment for violent and nonviolent drug-related offenses and prisons become privately owned and heavily funded, the prison population has grown rapidly, with black men the largest group in this population.[6] As systemic gendered racism leads to an ever-shrinking pool of "available" black men, some heterosexual black women find themselves competing with one another for male favor, attention, and relationships.[7]

Tension and conflict among black women is not a new phenomenon; rather, it is one that has historical roots in the ongoing systemic gendered racism of U.S. society.[8] Researchers cite struggles between upper- and lower-class black women dating back to the club movement of the nineteenth century, in which upper-class black women urged their lower-class counterparts to adopt mores of temperance and chastity in order to dispel white society's existing stereotypes of black women as sexually promiscuous and generally inferior.[9] In its present-day manifestations, competition and disagreement between black women occur within and across class borders, and can often foster environments of suspicion and strain within this group.

In some ways, the black beauty salon is a social space that directly challenges the ideologies of systemic gendered racism, which encourage adversarial, antagonistic relationships between black women. Owners talked specifically about their efforts to establish their salons as places that were welcoming, nurturing environments for black women in general, and for black women stylists in particular. Owners viewed their salons as places where they could offer stylists the necessary training, knowledge, and business management skills to eventually transition into entrepreneurship. I term this ethic of offering help, support, and guidance a "helping ideology."[10] This helping ideology is intended to facilitate black women stylists' transition to entrepreneurship and serves to challenge the messages of systemic gendered racism, which, again, encourage competition, mistrust, and suspicion among black women.

Many owners spoke of being guided by the helping ideology in their relationships with stylists. Lana probably offers the most interesting embodiment of this philosophy in practice. She explicitly tells stylists that eventually she expects them to use the knowledge they gain at her shop to pursue entrepreneurship:

> As long as they go work for themselves and not for someone else, it's cool. Because I feel somehow like a failure if they have to leave here and go work for someone else. It's like I didn't do my job. But I feel like if they go into business for themselves, I've shown them, helped them see the options there are for black women to really succeed in this field.

To make it unequivocally clear that she wants to encourage stylists to become owners, Lana also requires that her stylists attend mandatory workshops that she sponsors on money management, customer service, and business ethics so that they will have exposure to the knowledge she deems necessary for business ownership.

Miranda also embodies the helping ideology in her interactions with stylists. She worked for several years at a salon owned by another black woman, and credits her work experience there with giving her important tools for venturing out on her own:

> In the environment where I was at, watching and seeing how Miss Davis ran her business; basically it was another young lady going out at the time that I was going to leave, and she opened up a salon. So basically looking at them, the way they went about doing things, I kind of got an idea.

Miranda appreciated the assistance and the nurturing environment she experienced in Miss Davis's salon. Significantly, she seeks to pass this on to stylists that are in her employ:

> If they need somewhere to come, start out, this is basically I guess like a mission statement. I would like to give them a place to start out, somewhere where they can grow, feel comfortable, not feeling threatened, no competition, for them to build their clientele. And for them, once they grow, if they would like to get their own business one day, to do that. So basically, encourage them, teach them how to get their own shop, and to whatever they can dream, just go for it.

Miranda consciously seeks to establish the same supportive environment in her own salon that she benefited from in Miss Davis's. For her, the helping ideology is manifested in providing the guidance, nurture, and necessary information that will steer stylists toward entrepreneurship.

Interestingly, Miss Davis's daughter Denise was one of the owners interviewed for this study. Like Miranda and Lana, Denise also talks about working with other stylists to help them transition to business ownership:

> We've had young ladies that worked here go on to own shops. One young lady actually opened up a salon across the street. It was a breach of contract but we didn't bother her. I think she thought that because, you know, she was moving right over there that she would be in competition with us, but it didn't work out like that. She had to build her own client base and I did talk to her and tell her some of the things she needed to know to keep herself up, stay in business.

Again, the helping ideology compels these owners to encourage stylists to pursue entrepreneurship rather than remaining independent contractors.

Several of the owners interviewed for this study had previously worked as stylists for other owners in the sample. Tanisha and Greta worked for Lana before becoming salon owners, Maxine worked for Tanisha before pursuing entrepreneurship, and Miranda worked for Denise prior to establishing her own salon. This network of relationships itself is a testament to the success of the helping ideology in pushing stylists toward business ownership. However, not all of these stylist-turned-owners expressed the same level of commitment to or appreciation of the helping ideology. Lana and Tanisha's relationship best exemplifies the variation in ways that owners embodied the helping ideology.

Lana first met Tanisha at church after learning that Tanisha styled hair for many of the women in the congregation. Lana was impressed with Tanisha's natural talent and recruited her for employment as a stylist. Upon employment, however, Tanisha and Lana experienced some friction and personality clashes that Lana attributes primarily to Tanisha's youth. However, Tanisha remained at the salon for three years before moving on to open her own salon. Lana describes the progression of her relationship with Tanisha:

> I talked to her guidance counselor [to get permission for Tanisha to participate in work-study] and the counselor was like, "Oh, she has a learning disability, she's never going to be anything." Basically, her attitude was, "you take her because we don't know what else to do with her." And I worked with her, and it

wasn't easy. We had some challenges . . . but then I was like, "if I don't help the sister, what's going to happen to her?"

Lana's adherence to the helping ideology overrode her frustration with Tanisha's initial lack of professionalism and negative attitude. Lana's awareness of Tanisha's particular circumstances—an unsupportive guidance counselor and a learning disability—also compelled Lana to put the helping ideology into practice. She goes on to speak of Tanisha in glowing terms:

> I would hate for the others to hear me say this, but I think I'm the proudest of her because no one else had the challenges that she had and she has not only met her challenges, but she has surpassed all the others! She came back about two weeks ago and she made me cry. Every time I think about it I get teary-eyed, because she said, "I just wanted to thank you. Because everything I am today, you're responsible for that." I was like, "Oh my God! It really is worth it." It really, that made it all worthwhile, her saying that to me.

Lana was very aware of the positive impact that the helping ideology had on Tanisha's life. For Lana, the helping ideology solidified her commitment to Tanisha, despite a lack of professionalism and less than stellar work ethic.

Yet while Lana speaks of taking concrete, specific steps to put the helping ideology into practice and carries out this ideology in her interactions with Tanisha, Tanisha herself offers a more muted version of how she is influenced by the helping ideology. In contrast to owners like Miranda, Denise, and especially Lana, Tanisha employs the helping ideology very generally:

> I don't mind helping other people to do what I did, as long as they are not sneaky, envious, or jealous. I don't like that. But I'll tell people, "If you want to learn something from me, come to me!" I'll show you. I will help others because you can do the same thing that I do. If you need help, I'll help you. I don't mind.

Though Tanisha expresses a willingness to help other stylists, she does not specifically construct her salon as a place where she overtly attempts to encourage entrepreneurship among her stylists. She acknowledges that her help is always available but is not as effusive or forthright as Miranda or Lana.

While owners offer varying degrees of commitment to the helping ideology, it is important to consider the importance of this ideology as a contrast to the ideals of systemic gendered racism. Owners use the helping ideology as an ethic that infuses their relationships and interactions with stylists. By establishing their salons as places where they willingly offer stylists social support, advice, suggestions, and beneficial training to facilitate their transition to entrepreneurship, these owners challenge the dominant messages of gendered racism that encourage strife and contention among black women.

The emphasis on the helping ideology and fostering cooperation instead of competition is especially interesting given that these women actually are, strictly speaking, competitors. When Lana encourages her stylists to leave her salon to go into business for themselves, she is pushing them toward a course of action that actually works to her financial disadvantage. Recall that the terms of the relationship between stylists and owners are that stylists usually pay owners booth rent and are responsible for their own taxes, insurance, and other related costs. Therefore, Lana's desire to see her stylists become entrepreneurs actually incurs her financial loss, because she loses someone who has been paying her a monthly fee in booth rental. Similarly, Miranda's wish to give stylists a place to start before becoming entrepreneurs means that every time she succeeds in grooming a new salon owner, she simultaneously loses the income of that stylist's monthly booth rent.

I raised this apparent contradiction with some of the owners who were the most emphatic about the importance of pushing stylists to become entrepreneurs. Almost universally, they offered the same response: They weren't worried. Miranda told me, "There's more than enough business to go around. I might lose someone, but everyone is doing hair. I'll get someone else to fill that chair. And it's worth it to see these young ladies grow." Simply put, owners placed more value on the ability to help other black women achieve salon ownership than in the financial gains stylists brought them. Given the American emphasis on competitiveness, individualism, and gendered racist messages that exhort black women to see one another as rivals, this ethic is quite remarkable and incredibly noble.

Owners also recognized that the helping ideology offered them a way to enable other black women to increase their economic stability. In this way, they also were able to challenge the effects of systemic gendered racism. Many owners were well aware that salon ownership offered greater financial benefits than working as a stylist. When they employed the helping ideology to push their stylists toward entrepreneurship, they often did so with the awareness that stylists could maximize their earnings if they owned salons rather than simply working at salons. Donette stated, "Paying booth rent is what made the difference in my case. I could pay $400 a month to rent my booth, or pay $400 to rent my shop and hire stylists to pay booth rent to me. It just made sense."

Similarly, Lana asserted that, "This is really a field where black women can do well, and it's important to me that people know that and that they respect this industry." The knowledge that entrepreneurship offered greater financial returns than working as a stylist was part of the reason Donette and Lana championed the benefits of business ownership to their stylists.

Similarly, when discussing the ways Tanisha had blossomed as an entrepreneur, Lana said:

> She's doing so well. She just bought her third new car. She owns her own home. I know right now she is making more money than that teacher who said she would never be anything. She's doing so well, and she's beautiful! And this is the one, though, that they said wasn't going to be anything.

Part of Lana's pride stems from the fact that "the one . . . they said wasn't going to be anything" had been able to achieve a level of financial stability that likely surpassed those who initially doubted her. Owners often recognized that salon ownership would offer stylists greater economic security and consequently pushed stylists to pursue this route. Again, while they temporarily lost money by encouraging stylists to follow this road, this economic loss was less important than the personal gain that stemmed from helping another black woman.

Owners challenged systemic gendered racism by developing nurturing, supportive relationships with their stylists. Owners were motivated to cultivate these relationships by using the helping ideology—an ethic of encouragement, assistance, and mentorship that led owners to offer whatever aid they could to facilitate their stylists' professional development. The helping ideology therefore encouraged supportive relationships among black women, and pushed stylists to pursue the more economically rewarding business of entrepreneurship. As such, the helping ideology worked in opposition to systemic gendered racism in two important ways: It fostered cooperation among black women rather than the competition encouraged by systemic gendered racism, and encouraged stylists to pursue entrepreneurship as an alternative to the economic disadvantages systemic gendered racism produced in the larger society.

Creating a Safe Space for Black Women

In addition to the helping ideology, salon owners also challenged systemic gendered racism through their efforts to create a welcoming, secure space for black women in general. Owners explicitly sought to make their salons places that their predominantly black female clientele would consider a haven from any issues, problems, and unpleasantness of the outside world. As black women, these owners were well aware of the hardships black women faced in society. As such, they sought to establish their salons not only as places of business, but as "safe spaces" where black women could go to be rejuvenated, refreshed, and to escape temporarily from the pressures of the larger society.

Cultural critic bell hooks writes about the importance of the safe space for black women. She focuses on ways black women consciously created the home as a safe space, which she defines as "a . . . place where black people could affirm one another and by doing so heal many of the wounds inflicted by racist domination."[11] Other researchers have alluded to the concept of the safe space as essential for black women in coping with and resisting the oppression in various social institutions like the workplace or educational system.[12] A safe space enables black women to take time away from the indignities and pressures they experience in other settings, and to "restore . . . the dignity denied . . . on the outside in the public world."[13]

Black salon owners' efforts to establish their salons as havens for black women are reminiscent of this concept of safe spaces. As salon owners consciously strive to create environments that make black women feel like they are escaping from the tribulations of everyday life, they create safe spaces where black women are able to escape the pressures and stresses of systemic gendered racism. When owners seek to establish their salons as safe spaces, they challenge the systemic gendered racism black women encounter in society.

Owners talked about the importance of ensuring that the salon environment was one where black women could "get away." One way they focused on establishing this environment was through attention to aesthetic detail. Many owners were meticulous in making sure their salons were visually appealing, calming sanctuaries. Nadine's salon included a small fountain, jazz music, and a professional paint job. She stated:

> I spent a lot of money on the design in here. Personally, I think it's beautiful. I really wanted to make this a place where women could just come and relax and forget everything.

Others were well aware of the ways these environments had a positive impact on their clientele. Tanisha commented:

> When people come in, they're like, "it's pretty, it's really nice in here." And that makes me feel so good, but more important, it helps them to feel good.

Donette echoed these statements when she said:

> We have a bulletin board that allows our clients to know what's happening in town. We do cocktails, wine and cheese on some Saturdays once a month, I put up black art, things like that to just make the salon look really good, comfortable, really nice.

Finally, Lola stated:

> Not to brag or be conceited, but I feel like this is the closest I feel like black women have to a day spa. I will not have hardcore rap playing . . . this is supposed to be a serene environment.

By paying particular attention to the overall décor of their shops, these owners sought to create an environment that would make their black female clientele feel relaxed and calm.

Other owners made the salon a safe space for black women by constructing a friendly environment where all types of discussions thrived. Owners, customers, and stylists with whom I came into contact for this study often related that the beauty salon was a place where "anything goes," and any subject was open to discussion. One of Greta's customers echoed this when she stated:

> Coming in here is really like going to a psychiatrist's office. We talk about everything. Their lives, my life, and we share a lot. So that operates to our advantage because you meet people from different walks of life but you find out that you always have a lot in common. The disadvantage? I can't really say that there is one.

As this customer's statement suggests, owners were often able to establish a convivial environment so that open dialogue was commonplace at the beauty salon.

Charlene, another owner, voiced a similar statement about the interactions at the salon:

> Every day you talk to someone that you didn't talk to the day before. Every day it's something new, sharing information. We educate each other. With everyone in the salon, we develop friendships among ourselves. You see people's kids grow up because it is a diverse group. There may be four to six people waiting, everyone is doing something different, so you network and you end up talking about every possible thing.

Charlene also emphasizes the range of discussions that grow out of the various groups of people who attend the salon.

While no topics of conversation were off limits, certain subjects often took center stage at the salon. As a consequence of establishing an environment where customers, stylists, and owners could and did talk about everything, often discussions of issues that had particular salience to black women dominated the conversations. Because the owner, stylists, and customers were predominantly black women, when owners established an atmosphere where anything and everything was open to discussion, these topics were often discussed in such a way that they were framed through black women's particular experiences and perspectives.

During one visit to a salon for an interview, I overheard several stylists and customers engaged in a heated discussion about interracial relationships. These women discussed the difficulty finding "good black men" to date in the city, as well as black men's perceived willingness to date women who were not black and the extent to which they would feel comfortable dating interracially. While the subject of interracial dating could conceivably arise in numerous settings, in the salon these women were able to voice concerns and opinions about this issue that are largely informed by their position as black women. In other words, the specific focus on black men in interracial relationships and the issues associated with black women's options and motivations for dating interracially reflected the ways these women were free to discuss issues from their own perspectives.

Similarly, visiting another salon for an interview with the owner, I witnessed a conversation between a customer and a stylist concerning a popular black male R&B singer who had been accused of (and allegedly videotaped) engaging in sexual acts with a minor. These women discussed the veracity of these claims, the accuracy of the videotape in question, as well as the accolades this singer continued to receive despite the charges facing him. Again, this topic is not specific to the beauty salon but it is not surprising that it would emerge in this location, given that this singer frequently was marketed toward women, and given the staggering data that suggest that black women face extremely high rates of sexual assault.[14]

By establishing the salon as a soothing, peaceful environment where black women could discuss anything, salon owners were able to create a place where black women and their concerns, issues, and perspectives were fundamental rather than marginalized or ignored. Black women were able to view the salon as a relaxing alternative to the pressures and stressors they encountered in other social institutions. They also knew that the salon was a place where they were the focal point, rather than an afterthought. As such, they were able to make their most pressing issues and concerns the subject of discussion. By constructing the salon in this way, owners make it a safe space for black women.

The creation of the salon as a safe space allows black women owners to challenge systemic gendered racism by presenting their businesses as a haven from its debilitating effects. Systemic gendered racism in the larger society renders black women invisible, unimportant, and irrelevant. Owners challenge this by consciously establishing salons where black women are central, important, and necessary. They structure the décor of the salon with the idea that it should help their predominantly black female clientele relax comfortably in a soothing atmosphere. They create an environment where issues that matter and are important to black women are given attention and emphasis. These acts make the beauty salon a safe space, and thus allow owners to challenge the systemic gendered racism that marginalizes and devalues black women.

Valuing the Work

Given that gendered racism shapes the labor market and occupational opportunity, black women consequently experience not only economic disadvantage and exploitation, but also the devaluation of the work they perform. In jobs where black women are overrepresented, they are likely to experience not only low pay but also the sense that their work is undervalued, taken for granted, or marginal.[15] Domestic work, for example, is an occupation in which black women were overrepresented until the Civil Rights movement offered increased access to higher education and other occupational avenues. Research on black women domestic workers has demonstrated that these women often experienced dehumanizing treatment from their employers, including but not limited to the routine devaluation of their work.[16] To address this, these women relied on the strategy of "making [their] jobs good themselves"—they took pride in the fact that they worked hard and found value in their work, despite the fact that they were aware that employers rarely did so.[17]

As a consequence of systemic gendered racism, black women workers in other settings also find their work devalued. Many black women professionals report having to exhibit exceptional, near flawless work performance simply to have their work considered adequate and, even then, their white counterparts may surpass them despite a lesser degree of experience, success, and exemplary job performance.[18] Black professional women may find themselves trapped in a bind of low expectations, where white employers' perceptions of black women as less capable and intelligent make it difficult for these employers to recognize or accept outstanding work from their black women employees.[19]

Though the devaluation of black women's work exists in many work-places, black women salon owners were able to counteract this aspect of gendered racism by emphasizing the value and importance of the work they did. In contrast to gendered racist messages that suggest that black women's work is unimportant, trivial, or insignificant, salon owners challenged these negative dictates by highlighting the importance of their work and positively valuing it themselves.

The primary strategy owners used to highlight the importance of their work was to emphasize others' positive perceptions of their entrepreneurial work. Tanisha described the ways others perceived her status as an entrepreneur: "I'm young, and people are like, 'she got it going on, for real.' At their age—maybe I'm younger, and I'm further than a lot of people, and they envy me." Though Tanisha noted that sometimes the admiration she garnered from others could spill over into envy, she clearly felt that her status as a salon owner was something that elicited admiration from others.

Another owner, Chandra, was interviewed with one of her best friends, Samantha, who works for Chandra as a stylist. In their interview, Samantha spoke about the pride and respect she feels for Chandra as an entrepreneur:

> We're together all day long, but I am so proud of what she's doing. I always give praise to her and I'm like, "My best friend owns a shop." So that's the reward for me. My best friend owns a shop! Please! No, but seriously.

Samantha's sense of appreciation for Chandra's work was evident throughout the interview. Elsewhere, Donette talked about the support and excitement from her family and friends when she transitioned from working as a stylist to self-employment as a salon owner:

> Everybody was so willing to help you out. And they were really, all my friends, all my family members, were really excited. "You're going to open up your own salon, wow!" So that was easy, that was really easy.

Donette's sense that her family and friends were impressed by her decision to pursue entrepreneurship enabled her to view it in a positive light.

Other owners spoke of ways that they themselves valued the work they did and their position as entrepreneurs. Lana was perhaps the most forthright in her discussion of why and how she loved her work:

> I love this industry. I cannot think of anything else that I'd rather be doing. I don't know how to do anything else. . . . I do this because I love it. I do it to make money too, but the passion? That's something altogether different.

Lana continues to talk about the unsupportive guidance counselor who told her about Tanisha's learning disability and expected that she would be unsuccessful.

> That lady that sent Tanisha to me, in her head I'm sure she's thinking, "well, she can't do anything else to me but be a hairdresser." But you can't just be a hairdresser when you can't do anything else. You still need to have a brain, you still need to be educated, you still need to be articulate, you still need to, you know, be a lot of things, not *just* a hairdresser. You know, like it's dirty or something. That ain't something you do just cause you don't know how to do something else! You do this because you have a passion for it. Cause it's hard!

Lana's impassioned comments clearly articulated her awareness of how others may perceive work in the hair industry as something anyone can do, work that does not require any special skills or talents. However, Lana also explains the importance of education, poise, and presentation in being successful in the hair industry. She values the work that she does for the skills it requires and takes pride in her genuine passion for the industry.

Whether it is done by focusing on how they value the work or on the ways others admire it, salon owners' strategy of valuing their work challenges the gendered racist messages that minimize the importance of work done by black women. Like the aforementioned domestic workers, these women recognized the importance of giving value to their work as a contrast to the devaluation it endured from others. Though in some cases salon owners were aware that others held negative or less flattering perceptions of the work they did, in general, these owners held their work in very high regard. They took pride in their status as entrepreneurs and appreciated the success they had as business owners. This appreciation for their work challenges gendered racist ideals that suggest that the work black women do is unimportant and unvalued.

Reproducing Gendered Racism

Businesses in the racial enclave economy not only challenge aspects of gendered racism, they also reproduce some forms of gendered racism. Within the hair salon, gendered racism was reproduced most frequently in the area of perceptions of other black women customers and stylists. Even though owners challenged systemic gendered racism by pushing stylists toward economic stability through salon ownership and establishing their businesses as safe havens that concentrated on meeting black women's needs, in some cases, owners' attitudes and views of black women in the salon were shaped by stereotypes about black women that are an integral part of the lexicon of systemic gendered racism.

Blacks as "Ghetto"

One of the key ways owners reinforced gendered racism was through language that established certain behaviors, attitudes, and actions as being "ghetto." This phrasing surfaced in many interviews, always in contrast to the atmosphere or clientele that owners were attempting to draw into their salons. Describing behavior or individuals as "ghetto" usually meant that they were being loud, tacky, wild, and rude. Though unspoken, this was a label usually used to refer to other black women who might be noisy, attract unwanted negative attention, or, in the words of one owner, "bring drama."

Clarice, quoted at the start of this chapter, is an owner who spoke candidly about this issue. She was one of the few owners who, when working as a stylist, had worked in both predominantly black and predominantly white salons. Clarice stated that she had been able to fit in at both salons with relative ease. However, she contrasted her own experience to those of other black women she encountered: "Some women will really get into trouble because their shop is, I hate to say this, but it's ghetto. And their shops are ghetto because they're ghetto. That only attracts a certain type of business." Other owners decried any association with things or people that appeared ghetto. Tanisha contrasted her salon's atmosphere with that of others that were more ghetto as a way of explaining her salon's appeal to potential stylists:

> One stylist was in an unprofessional atmosphere and she wanted to try something different. She said that she liked the way my salon was. It's small, it's intimate, no loudness, no gossiping, I don't have men coming in and out of here, so she said she wanted the change. She needed a different atmosphere, so that's how I got her. And the other stylist, I got her through word of mouth. She came down here, she heard it was a nice salon, a nice atmosphere, none of that loud talking, *none of them ghetto people*. That's how I got her. [*Emphasis added.*]

Tanisha clearly sets up the contrast between her "small, intimate" salon and the "loud talking, ghetto people" who inhabit less desirable shops.

Carrie, another owner, described the challenges that come from having a salon associated with this image:

> I would prefer a middle-class, professional clientele, out of high school, and mature. You can be twenty-one but appear twenty-eight, or older. It does have a negative effect on the business, having this type of clientele. You can't

change people, and this place is sort of in the ghetto, so that's what I end up with.

Here, Carrie refers to her "ghetto" clients as being a product of their environment. However, she still views this as a drawback to her business.

Other owners similarly describe these types of salons as "loud" or "wild," often ascribing negative values to such places. Maxine is one owner who spoke disparagingly about these salons:

> The clientele will be like your personality. I've seen some places that were loud and wild, operators don't get along, and everyone is bickering. That's not good for the clients because it doesn't make them feel good. It just sets up a really ghetto environment. That's not what we have here.

Again, Maxine identifies the noise and level of activity as indicators of a more "ghetto" establishment and contrasts that to what she establishes in her salon.

Owners' descriptions of certain environments and individuals as "ghetto" reproduce systemic gendered racist ideals that attribute certain negative behaviors to blacks. Sociologists have suggested that in the post–Civil Rights era, racial language becomes coded and covert, so that terms like "urban," "quotas," or "inner-city" convey racial messages without using overtly racial terminology.[20] In interviews with these salon owners, "ghetto" became another such terminology for referring to blacks who exhibited behaviors that were considered uncouth or unappealing. Black women in particular were coded as ghetto if they were too loud, dramatic, and provoked too much negative attention. Yet this coded language (and the ideals behind it) reinforces the ideology of systemic gendered racism that applies negative, racially specific messages to certain behaviors.

The Hip-Hop Crowd

Owners also reinforced aspects of gendered racism by applying other stereotypes about black women to potential employees and customers. In addition to the imagery of certain behaviors among blacks as ghetto, the stereotype that surfaced most frequently was the image of black women as being part of what owners termed "the hip-hop crowd." This terminology was generally heard among older owners in their forties and fifties, who applied this label to younger women whose behaviors, attitudes, and styles of dress seemed to approximate owners' assessments of women's actions in hip-hop music

videos. Owners were loath to hire stylists or market their services toward customers who appeared to be members of the hip-hop crowd, and spoke at
length about the adverse effects these types of black women had on their
business.

Charlene gave one of the most specific examples of the behavior and
attitudes of women who were part of the hip-hop crowd. She described
them as:

> You know, those girls who come in late, [with] certain behaviors . . . cursing,
> carrying on, dressed like those girls in the videos. That is not professional.

Similarly, as Lola described her efforts to create an atmosphere of comfort for
her black female clientele, she juxtaposed this by describing the type of stylist who would undermine these efforts:

> I will not have hardcore rap playing, or that type of person to assist me. And if
> I did have that type, hopefully I could change her. Those types dwindle. As
> clients mature, they look for something different.

Another owner, Donette, expounded further:

> Some of those types, they do have the slow thing going on. They want to play
> the loud music, the chit-chatting on the phone while the customer is sitting
> there. Yeah, we haven't worked that out yet.

These owners felt that black women stylists who were part of the hip-hop
crowd would bring undesirable values and atmosphere into their shop. As
such, they took pains to avoid hiring women who appeared to fit this image.

Other owners tried to avoid attracting a customer base that resembled the
hip-hop crowd. Maxine stated:

> You attract what you are, and in places where the customers are all ghetto and
> loud, people who are like that fit right into that scene. The customers that
> come in here, they know when they come in if this is the place for them. And
> if they want that, I don't want to say better, but that nicer atmosphere, they'll
> come here. You know when you walk in if its right for you.

As Maxine explained, the clientele that she was able to establish sets an immediate tone for prospective customers. In her case, she takes pride in the
fact that her clientele does not convey a sense of familiarity to the hip-hop
crowd.

Lola also talked about trying to avoid drawing a hip-hip crowd as her primary client base:

> I have more of a professional clientele. Lawyers, doctors, social workers, because I can't deal with people on a certain level. Sometimes I do, but then sometimes I don't. Sometimes people think that, oh, she's too bourgie or whatever. No, that's not it. I just look at people that pay my bills, and I need people that have jobs, and I cater to them. I sure enough do, and I may show favoritism, but they [are] the people that pay my bills. I'm not knocking down younger people, college kids, or whatever. I take them too, but they can be . . . I don't want a crowd of just the hip-hoppers. I just, I cater to a certain clientele, as far as professional women.

Lola explicitly sought to avoid what she described as younger people and those on a certain level. She contrasted the young "hip-hoppers" to the more professional crowd that she really wanted to attract. Lola went on to echo Maxine when she stated:

> You will know if you fit here. This is not for everybody because they are not at that peak yet, they are not at that level. So a lot of people don't fit here, just as like, clients. You feel out of place because you're not there yet.

Again, there is an effort to avoid the hip-hop crowd as the main customer base, for fear of what implications this will have for business.

Interestingly, Chandra was one owner who felt that her clientele was primarily comprised of people who could be considered members of the hip-hop crowd. She had many complaints about the customers and several of her stylists, and described the atmosphere in her shop by saying:

> We got this kind of "homey" thing here. We service the "homies" and the "yo-whites." The "yo-type" ones who want to be black, or the black ones who are like, "Homegirl, I don't have all the money now, but I got you when we go to the club." No, you got me now because I have to go pay my babysitter when I leave. It's just crazy. My clientele, is, it's different ages, some different races, but mostly, it's street hustlers, you know.

Though Chandra relies on the clientele that other salon owners try to avoid, she shares their frustration with the unreliability and negative atmosphere she perceives among this group.

The stereotypes among owners that some black women tend to be "ghetto," or part of "the hip-hop crowd," represent ways that owners may reproduce the gendered racism of the larger society. Owners utilize racialized stereotypes of blacks as ghetto or hip-hoppers to inform their interactions with potential customers and employees. It is important to point out that, in this context, these racialized stereotypes are also classed and gendered. The perception of certain blacks behaving or speaking in a way that is considered "ghetto" is a specifically class-based stereotype that refers to primarily working and lower-class blacks who are noisy and uncontrollable. Similarly, the stereotype of certain women being part of the hip-hop crowd is a gendered stereotype of black women who curse and dress provocatively. When owners employ these stereotypes as a manner of weeding out certain black women as stylists or customers, they reproduce the systemic gendered racism of the larger society that creates and perpetuates these stereotypes.

These stereotypes are particularly significant as a tool of systemic gendered racism because they promote a key aspect of its ideology—the message of black cultural inferiority. The idea of black cultural inferiority has long-term, historic roots and has been particularly useful in perpetuating systemic racism. [21] As far back as slave times, blacks were depicted as being culturally or inherently inferior to whites. This argument was used to rationalize black enslavement, resurfaced in the 1970s in the Moynihan Report, and has contemporary manifestations in the view that blacks' disadvantaged position in the labor market and disproportionate representation in the criminal justice system is best explained by their inherently deviant cultural values, rather than any continuing, institutionalized racial inequality.[22] The view of black cultural inferiority suggests that blacks in general are lazy and is gendered in its implication that black men are prone to violent crime while black women are emasculating matriarchs who maintain an inordinate (and inappropriate) level of control over black men, families, and communities. The focus on these stereotypical attributes of black culture obscures the impact of past and continuing discrimination, as well as the embeddedness of racial inequality in most American social institutions.

When salon owners apply coded racial terms such as "ghetto" and speak of avoiding those in "the hip-hop crowd," they reproduce the ideology of systemic gendered racism, specifically, the principle of black cultural inferiority. Furthermore, when they act on these stereotypes to avoid working with those whom they label in this way, owners reinforce some of the very aspects of systemic gendered racism that they challenge with their other behaviors. In particular, they buttress the tenets of systemic gendered racism, which enforce divisiveness among black women and reinforce systemic gendered racist ideologies that justify labor market inequalities by blaming inherent cultural values.

Summary

As a business in the racial enclave economy, the hair salon both reproduces and challenges aspects of gendered racism. Gendered racism that promotes competition, facilitates economic instability, and marginalizes black women and their work is challenged by the owners' tendency to employ the helping ideology to help black women experience financial security, and their focus and emphasis on creating a safe space where black women's comfort is paramount. However, the challenges to systemic gendered racism are not ubiquitous in the racial enclave economy. Even while aspects of racial enclave businesses rebut certain manifestations of gendered racism, owners are still subjected to gendered racism in the larger society and may simultaneously reproduce some of its tenets within the enclave. The primary way this reproduction takes place is through owners' stereotypes and generalizations, which implicitly uphold the ideas of cultural inferiority that are a key part of the ideological component of systemic gendered racism.

On a broader scale, the reproduction and contestation of gendered racism can be interpreted as tension between the dominant frame of systemic gendered racism and an available counterframe. Systemic racism is gendered; so too are the white racist frames that legitimize it and the counterframes that challenge it. Owners' efforts to value their work, to create safe spaces for black women, and to help other women achieve the financial and social benefits of entrepreneurship are a counterframe to the systemic gendered racist ideology that black women and the work that they do are unappreciated and worthless. The helping ideology in particular is a counterframe to the systemic gendered racist ideology that black women should see one another as enemies or competitors rather than as comrades who collectively face oppressive conditions. This counterframe is gendered in that it specifically addresses the negative, systemic racist messages that abound about black women—that they are untrustworthy, mean, and cold.[23] By actively working to help other black women experience economic improvement at the expense of their own profit margins, these owners clearly counter systemic gendered racist messages about black women's meanness.

Yet while owners endorse this counterframe, they simultaneously accept some aspects of the dominant white racist frame that legitimizes systemic racism. The same owners who employed counterframes to challenge systemic gendered racist ideas of black women also supported and in some cases even made business decisions based on racist frames of black cultural inferiority. They interpreted certain behaviors through the lens of the white racist frames that legitimize racist hierarchies and unequal treatment of blacks. In these cases, white racist frames justified biased treatment of other black women, as owners talked about conscious efforts to avoid hiring or even attracting customers or employees whose behaviors could be conceived as "ghetto" or too "hip-hop."

The diametrical tension between the counterframes and the white racist frames these owners simultaneously employed is both interesting and problematic. Owners' use of counterframes allows them to combat certain white racist frames and to affirm black women, even going so far as to provide opportunities for economic advancement. Yet the extent to which they use counterframes is circumscribed by their acceptance of traditional white racist frames that legitimize discriminatory treatment of blacks. None of the owners articulated or acknowledged any contradiction in their convictions that the hair industry was a way to combat the challenging experiences black women faced in society, and their endorsement of some of the very stereotypes that constrain opportunities for black women.

This conundrum represents the perniciousness of systemic gendered racism and the ideological frames that support it. Although some work has suggested that blacks, over time, have developed sophisticated counterframes that critique systemic racism, other research suggests that blacks also fall prey to internalizing some of systemic racism's messages and frames.[24] The owners interviewed here employ a complicated interplay of white racist frames *and* counterframes. Both work in tandem to shape owners' beliefs and legitimize their actions.

Owners' susceptibility to white racist frames also illustrates the pervasiveness of systemic gendered racism as an institutional issue rather than an individual one. Much of the current popular thinking about racism today suggests that it is present only among very few people and consists of a set of negative personal views that can be changed with education. Conventional wisdom today thus suggests that anyone, regardless of race, can be racist should they hold or espouse negative viewpoints about another racial group. Recent sociological research on race has debunked this view, arguing that power relations and the presence of racism in various institutions present race as a larger structural phenomenon rather than an individual issue of a few bad apples.[25]

Owners' internalizations of certain white racist frames complicate this picture. Most sociological research on race suggests that racial minorities cannot be racist because as a group, they lack the institutional power to deny opportunities and advantages to other racial groups. I myself agree with this framework. But what happens when minorities like these salon owners *are* in a position to withhold social, economic, or political rewards to others based on race? Does this make them racist? These owners candidly acknowledged that they do shy away from hiring certain blacks, but I contend that simply labeling them "racist" obscures the broader sociological issues at hand: While these women may work to deny opportunities to certain black women, they are doing so in conjunction with a racist framework that was created and maintained by whites to benefit whites, and ultimately works to perpetuate black women's disadvantage. Though owners do have (limited) power to keep occupational and economic opportunities from other black women, this phenomenon is more accurately represented by describing their endorsement of white racist frames than by labeling these women as racist actors.

CHAPTER SIX

Ethnic Divisions in the Racial Enclave

The customers say [the workers] don't know how to do customer service, that they don't respect the customers. So, that can be very hard.

—Mariane, 34

Mariane is a small woman who speaks very softly, barely above a whisper. When she showed me into her high-ceilinged, three-room salon for her interview, she seemed almost nervous about speaking with me. However, she was forthcoming if not effusive, telling me about immigrating to the United States from Senegal, West Africa, in her early twenties, her extended family in America, the classes she took at a local university, and how her husband helped her with her work as a salon owner. In ways that I will discuss in this chapter, Mariane's experiences mirrored those of black American women interviewed for this project. However, her ethnic identity as an African woman, rather than an American, created important differences between her experiences in the racial enclave economy and those of black American women.

Up to now, I have focused on the experiences of black women salon owners who were raised in the United States and identify as African American. This focus is necessary, given the central claim of this book that the tendency to overemphasize ethnic groups when studying entrepreneurship obscures the significant role race plays in structuring racial minorities' experiences with business ownership. However, it is important to consider that racial categories include a multiplicity of ethnicities. As such, this chapter explores the experiences of ethnic groups within the racial enclave economy. Here, I explore ethnic differences among women entrepreneurs in the racial enclave economy. I assess similarities and differences in the ways systemic gendered racism influences the entrepreneurial experiences of African American and black ethnic women business owners.

The difference between race and ethnicity is primarily one of cultural origin. Race refers to obvious physical characteristics like skin color or hair texture, while ethnicity refers to specific cultural traits. Consequently, the racial label "black" can include Haitians, Jamaicans, Bahamians, and immigrants from various African countries. Even those who may identify ethnically as Puerto Ricans, Dominicans, or Cubans may be racially categorized as black depending on their physical appearance.

This chapter draws on intensive interviews with five women salon owners of various ethnic groups. All owners were born and raised in African countries and immigrated to the United States as adults. Additionally, they all owned salons that only offered braiding services.[1] At these salons, customers could choose to have their hair braided in a variety of styles. These braided styles are most common among black women, so these salons were even less likely than others to attract the occasional white, Asian American, or Latina customer, and rarely, if ever, serviced men of any racial or ethnic group. Though the small number of black ethnic women interviewed here in no way provides a representative or generalized sample, these women's experiences as salon owners provide an important window into the manifestations of ethnic differences within the racial enclave economy.

Common Themes

Several common themes emerged from black ethnic salon owners. Like black American entrepreneurs, issues of family and work were central to their entrepreneurial experiences. These issues are also linked to the reality of systemic gendered racism. However, important differences are reflected in the ways these issues arise among black ethnic salon owners.

For black ethnic salon owners, family played a very important role in the process of business ownership. Unlike black American salon owners who were able to benefit from important social and economic capital they accumulated as a result of working as stylists for other black American women owners, black ethnic owners followed a different path to entrepreneurship. All of the black ethnic owners interviewed for this study came to own their shop through a male relative. Often, a husband, brother, or other male relative preceded them to America and opened the salon. When these men ultimately pursued other work options or education, they simply gave the sa-lons to their female relatives to own and manage. Family ties were thus very important in black ethnic women's transition to entrepreneurship.

Tabia is a 28-year-old immigrant from Guinea. She described her tran-sition to working in the salon and subsequent ownership, stating, "I wanted to come and help my brother. He owned this shop first but then he went to another job. So now I'm here and I do braids here." Since Tabia's brother gave her the salon, she sidestepped many of the difficulties black American owners experienced upon transitioning to entrepreneur-ship, like locating financing.

Senait reported a similar account of becoming an entrepreneur. When asked why she decided to open a hair salon, she stated, "This was my brother's shop. We just got this shop, me and my husband, like three months ago. . . . My brother bought it but now he is going to school so he gave it to us." Like Tabia, Senait was able to take over ownership of the shop from her relative, which undoubtedly eased some aspects of the shift to entrepreneur-ship.

Tasha, a salon owner from Togo, took over her salon from her uncle. Tasha said:

> My uncle had this shop first. I came here after he had had it for a few years. He wanted to go to school because he wanted to get a degree and make more money. So, he gave me this shop when he went.

Once again, male kin play a crucial role in becoming a salon owner. These men are able to establish and maintain salons, then pass them along to fe-male relatives when they are ready to pursue other options. This benefits black ethnic women who become salon owners because they are able to take over a salon that is already operational, rather than building one from the ground up.

Family also became an important source of labor for black ethnic salon owners. Unlike black American owners, who did not consciously seek to hire family, black ethnic salon owners often relied heavily or exclusively on ex-tended family for the necessary labor. Fatima is a 30-year-old immigrant from Cameroon who stated: "It's good working with family. If it's busy, you can call somebody to come and help you."

When asked if working with her family presented any difficulties, she replied, "That depends. That's the, you know, some people's difference. I never, I don't know about that problem. Maybe some have that problem. For mine, I'm okay." For Fatima, family presented an important source of necessary labor that enabled her to meet the demands of customers in the salon. She did not consider it problematic to work with relatives.

In several cases, these same family members worked for the original male owner and simply stayed on when this owner gave the salon to a female relative. In these cases, these salons were very much family businesses, as they remained owned and staffed by family members, even if an owner decided to leave. Senait's experience reflected this:

> I just moved here a few months ago [but] it was a family shop. I was working with my sister. My other two sisters, they go back home but they'll be back here next January.

Her sisters initially worked for her brother; they now work for Senait as the owner.

Black ethnic salon owners' reliance on family labor parallels research on other ethnic entrepreneurship endeavors that suggests family labor is crucial to the success of businesses in the ethnic enclave.[2] Gender and marital status play a significant role in men's entrepreneurship in the ethnic enclave; indeed, women's participation as family members is often crucial to men's entrepreneurial success in ethnic enclave businesses.[3] Similarly, family networks are an important source of labor for middleman minority entrepreneurs.[4] For black ethnic women, family ties are crucial in both facilitating business ownership and in providing the necessary labor supply for these businesses.

Black ethnic salon owners did not rely solely on family for labor, however. Though they drew most of their labor force from extended family, in some cases black ethnic owners hired outside the family. In these cases, they were most likely to employ co-ethnics. At Senait's salon, the only employee who was not a family member was a close friend of hers who had also emigrated from Nigeria. At Tasha's salon, she employed several family members and co-ethnic employees who were not relatives. As with Senait, however, she knew her employees prior to hiring them. "I met [my employees] at the cultural center. So I knew them when I first got here. And then when I needed people to work here, I hired them." Tasha pointedly hired co-ethnics that she knew to work in her shop. Consequently, her salon was completely staffed by co-ethnics she knew well or extended family members.

The reliance on co-ethnic labor also mirrors other studies of ethnic groups' entrepreneurship. Ethnic solidarity is important to many forms of ethnic entrepreneurship. Within ethnic enclaves, ethnic solidarity forms an important bond between employer and employee.[5] Ethnic solidarity motivates employers in the ethnic enclave to hire co-ethnics, who have greater employment opportunities within the enclave. Among black ethnic salon owners, ethnic solidarity compels these women to hire other ethnic women to work in their salons. By and large, owners consciously sought to staff their salons with black women who shared their ethnic background.

The final theme that surfaced repeatedly in interviews was the discussion of intra-racial or inter-ethnic tension between black ethnic women who owned or worked at the salon and their black American customers. Black ethnic salon owners spoke frequently of the difficulties they faced when interacting with their black American clientele. They also described encounters where their employees experienced conflict with black American women customers. Note that in braiding salons, black ethnic women owners and stylists are mainly servicing black American women customers. The conflicts that arise, then, are between black women of different ethnic backgrounds.

Tension with customers stemmed from a variety of sources. Owners attributed problems with customers to various factors. For example, Fatima identified the language barrier as a key part of the trouble she initially had with some customers. She stated:

> It was a little hard at first because I came in and I start this job and I work a little bit harder because I had to learn the language. Sometimes the customers, they did not like it if I couldn't understand them.

In Fatima's case, once she became more fluent in English, she was able to relate and interact more easily with her clientele.

In contrast, Senait contextualized the difficulties interacting with clients as a customer service issue. She acknowledged:

> Sometimes the way they treat the customer, it's not right. Then customers complain about the workers. They say they don't know how to do customer service, they don't respect the workers.

While Senait observed what customers consider disrespectful treatment from some employees, she considered herself fortunate to have been able to avoid such issues:

> I'm lucky. Most of my customers, they're very nice to me. Sometimes you find some that are very, very hard, but you have to deal with that person. They are a customer . . . and my husband is helping me a lot with how to take care of your customers, how to make them happy.

For Senait, customer service (or lack thereof) is the issue that creates strain between clients and workers.

Finally, Tasha introduced a third source of discontent between customers and staff. She claimed that customers attempted to take advantage of workers by trying to get more for less:

> They don't respect the prices. I hate that they always complain about what it costs. I have the hair here so they don't have to buy it, so my prices seem a little higher, but really it's the same because it includes the cost of the hair. Why don't they understand that? Why do they always want me to work for less?

At Tasha's salon, like most braiding shops, she offered styles that usually required hair extensions. Unlike most braiding shops, Tasha kept the hair extensions on the premises so that customers would not have to buy the hair themselves. However, she then passed on the costs of the hair by adding it on to customers' prices. As she described, this strategy often upset customers who felt that her prices were too high. In turn, Tasha grew irritated with customers and what she perceived as a tendency to try to take advantage of her and her staff.

The intra-racial, inter-ethnic tension that these owners describe is not without precedent. Studies of ethnic entrepreneurship often depict examples of conflict between ethnic entrepreneurs and the larger host society.[6] Certain paradigms of ethnic entrepreneurship are likely to incur hostility from the host society. As go-betweens who provide services to the masses, middleman minority entrepreneurs often experience tensions from the masses that comprise their clientele. The conflict between some African Americans and Korean immigrant middleman minority entrepreneurs is an example of this.[7]

Strained relationships between black Americans and black ethnics have also been documented elsewhere. In her research on ethnic conflicts among blacks, sociologist Mary Waters has established that black Americans and black ethnic groups may each reiterate or internalize stereotypes about the other group.[8] She finds that black ethnic groups may distance themselves from black Americans based on the perception that black Americans are lazy, do not want to work, and complain too much about racism. Conversely, black Americans may perceive black ethnic groups as snobby and condescending. Though both are considered members of the same racial group, ethnic tensions still exist and can be difficult to bridge.

Thus, the common themes cited by black ethnic salon owners in some ways parallel the experiences of other ethnic groups who pursue entrepreneurship. Like middleman minority and ethnic enclave entrepreneurs, black ethnic women in the racial enclave economy draw heavily from kin networks and co-ethnics as an important source of labor. They also experience conflict with others outside their ethnic group, usually in the form of hostility from their black American clientele. However, I suggest that despite the similarities to some aspects of middleman minority and ethnic enclave entrepreneurship, these women's entrepreneurial ventures are best categorized as part of the racial enclave economy. Their status as immigrants does inform their entrepreneurial experiences in ways that mirror those of other ethnic groups. Ultimately, however, these women are still subjected to systemic gendered racism in ways that other ethnic groups may not be. The effects of systemic gendered racism profoundly shape their entrepreneurial experiences in many ways, and render their work part of the racial enclave economy.

Systemic Gendered Racism

Despite their ethnic identity and status as immigrants, gendered racism impacted black ethnic women's entrepreneurial activity in several ways. In some cases, gendered racism shaped black ethnic women's experiences in the racial enclave in ways that paralleled the experiences of black American women. Gendered racism also structured black ethnic women's entrepreneurship in ways that diverged from those of black American women. Consequently, while ethnic differences are present among black women in the racial enclave economy, ultimately systemic gendered racism plays an important role in entrepreneurial work.

Gendered racism is not uniquely American but in many cases permeates social policy and ideology on an international scale. The experiences of black ethnic women demonstrate that gendered racism is a global, rather than a domestic, phenomenon. Western policies advanced by the International Monetary Fund (IMF) and the World Bank that encourage free trade with minimal rights, protection, and standards for workers ultimately exacerbate the growing numbers of the world's poor, who are primarily women and children of color. As Barker and Feiner assert in their assessment of the impact of economic policy on women and children, "export-led industrialization strategies require significant pools of women willing to work for low wages at monotonous, often hazardous tasks."[9]

Western assumptions about race, gender, and economic progress are embedded in these types of policies. Consequently, many women in various African countries—and women in countries in the African Diaspora like Haiti, the Dominican Republic, or Jamaica—are profoundly affected by development plans that seek to push certain models of advancement. One micro-level effect of these policies is that black women internationally, re-gardless of ethnic identity, find themselves invested in micro-enterprise schemes. In micro-enterprise businesses, women may make and sell sundry items like rugs, jewelry, or even food, to tourists.[10] Changing economies, un-stable political processes, and policies of financial institutions all contribute to a global economy that leaves women in African countries with few op-portunities for financial stability.[11] As such, systemic gendered racism on a global scale creates a large population of black women who are unskilled, have limited access to education, and have minimal job opportunities (and those they do have are unlikely to lift them out of poverty). These dismal choices often facilitate African women's immigration to America, under the belief that there will be greater options and better opportunities than those they face in their native countries.

Once these women immigrate to America and are established as salon owners, systemic gendered racism continues to affect their entrepreneurial experiences. Like black American women salon owners, gendered racism provides these black ethnic women with a market for their services. As dis-cussed at length in chapter 3, a key ideological component of systemic gen-dered racism is the idea that black women are unattractive, undesirable, and unappealing. Black ethnic women are able to meet a need of this market by providing beauty services to other black women.

Interestingly, in visiting the braiding salons owned by black ethnic women, I noticed that their clientele was often younger than those in salons owned by black American women. Black ethnic owners acknowledged this and commented that their client base was often comprised of younger, semi-professional women. Senait stated: "Customers are around 25, maybe the oldest ones are 35. Most of them are in school. Some work in an office as sec-retaries." Tasha noticed a similar trend among her customers: "A lot of them go to State University. Not many older women come here."

I suspect that the young, semiprofessional customer base these women are able to attract also reflects specific contours of gendered racism. The popu-larity and mainstream acceptability of braided hairstyles is a relatively recent phenomenon. During the black power movement in the 1970s, many black American women began to wear natural hair as a way of rejecting gendered racist ideologies that suggested that women's primary goal was to be beauti-ful, and that straight hair was a prerequisite for meeting this goal.[12] Older black Americans may be more likely to consider black women's hair in its natural state an unappealing or even offensive violation of beauty norms.[13] Systemic gendered racism thus may shape black ethnic women's access to an available market, by negatively influencing older black women's ideas about the appropriateness or appeal of braided hair.

The fact that black ethnic women attracted a customer base of mostly semiprofessional black American women may also be indicative of particular aspects of gendered racism. Though braided hairstyles on adult black American women have become more mainstream since the black power movement, they have not yet become universally acceptable in all sectors. Organizations that pride themselves on maintaining a more traditional culture, or occupations that require interactions with conservative clients, may not welcome black women employees with braided hairstyles in professional or high-ranking positions. Black women in such positions speak frequently of the pressures they experience to assimilate and to avoid appearing "too black."[14] For these women, wearing braided hairstyles may simply be unfeasible given the organizational culture and demands of the professional workplace. The presence of gendered racism in professional workplaces, then, can serve to constrain the market black ethnic women entrepreneurs may reasonably expect to reach.

On a macro level, systemic gendered racism creates a supply of black ethnic women with few marketable skills but also works to constrain the demand for the skills these women do possess. Like their black American women counterparts, systemic gendered racism puts black ethnic women entrepreneurs in a position where work in the racial enclave economy is one of few options for economic stability. Gendered racism also shapes black ethnic women entrepreneurs' access to clients, as is also the case with black American women entrepreneurs in the racial enclave. Importantly, however, systemic gendered racism narrows the market for black ethnic women's services.

Intra-Racial Tension: The Reproduction of Gendered Racism

Micro-level interactions within black ethnic women's salons reflect the existence of gendered racism also. One of the key themes that surfaced in the interviews with these women involved the tensions they noted between themselves and their black American customers. As discussed earlier, they ascribed these tensions to various factors including the existence of a language barrier, clients' desire to take advantage of owners, or staff members' rudeness toward customers. The strained relationship that black ethnic owners sometimes experienced with their black American clients also reflects the influence of gendered racism.

Racial enclave economies are defined, in part, by the simultaneous reproduction and contestation of systemic gendered racism within the business establishments. Black American women reproduce gendered racism through their reliance on stereotypes of certain black women, even as they challenge systemic gendered racism with their willingness to create safe spaces for black women and to help other black women experience economic security. Within the racial enclave economy, black ethnic women also participate in the reproduction and contestation of systemic gendered racism. Yet these processes produce different outcomes than those observed for black American women.

The strained relationship between black American and black ethnic women contributes to the reproduction of gendered racism. As is the case with black American women, systemic gendered racism encourages black women to view each other with hostility, suspicion, and mistrust. The experiences of black ethnic women within the racial enclave economy suggest that such views may coalesce along ethnic lines. Thus, the perception that the tensions between black American and black ethnic women stem from the former's attempt to take advantage of the latter are significant when viewed in the context of systemic gendered racism. This viewpoint ultimately upholds gendered racist ideologies of black women as untrustworthy and conniving.[15]

Tensions between these two groups are reciprocal. In some interviews, black ethnic women entrepreneurs also felt that their black American customers were rude or unpleasant. Tabia stated:

> Sometimes my client can be very mean; they say they want to sue if they don't think I did their hair right. It's not all the clients but there are some that can be very mean.

Discourteous behavior toward black ethnic salon owners also functions to reproduce ideals of systemic gendered racism. When black American women treat black ethnic women poorly, this behavior reinforces negative messages about black women that are implicit in the ideals of systemic gendered racism.

While tensions between black ethnic and black American women serve to reproduce gendered racism, black ethnic women's relationships with employees also challenge systemic gendered racism. Much like black American women, black ethnic women consciously seek out other black women to staff their salons. Tasha described hiring other women she knew from a cultural center, Senait employed family members and friends in her salon, and Tabia reported contacting friends to help her braid when she was busy. By providing necessary employment to other black women, these owners challenge the systemic gendered racism that economically exploits black women and channels them into low-wage work.

Importantly, however, black ethnic women limit their efforts to other black ethnic women. These black ethnic women entrepreneurs do not hire other black women indiscriminately; they hire other black women from their particular ethnic group. None of the women interviewed suggested or even implied that they would refuse to hire black American stylists but, in reality, each owner employed only other co-ethnic women. Thus, while these women challenge gendered racism by offering occupational opportunity to black women, this assistance is limited to black women of their ethnic group.

The contours of this occupational assistance are not, fundamentally, so different from black American salon owners' challenges to systemic gendered racism. Black ethnic women may concentrate their employment opportunities among co-ethnics but so too do black American salon owners who tend to hire other black American women. Ultimately, both black ethnic and black American owners challenge systemic gendered racism by deliberately seeking to employ other black women. Yet the reproduction of intra-racial divisions may undermine this particular contestation of systemic gendered racism.

Black ethnic women's efforts to offer employment to fellow co-ethnics may, however, create latent dysfunctions that their black American counterparts escape. Black ethnic women's efforts to hire co-ethnic employees may undermine the salon's potential to function as a safe space for clientele. Given that black ethnic owners themselves admit that strained relationships sometimes exist between their co-ethnic employees and black American customers, it is feasible that owners' efforts to employ fellow ethnics may exacerbate the tension between staff and customers. This inter-ethnic tension may hinder these salons from functioning as safe spaces in the same way that salons owned by black American women do.

Indeed, during visits to black ethnic women's braiding salons, I rarely observed the camaraderie or heard the constant discussion that was characteristic of black American women's salons. Black ethnic owners and employees were more likely to talk among themselves (and sometimes did so in their first language) while customers read magazines, watched television, or simply sat patiently waiting for the stylist to finish. At Tasha's salon, she and two other stylists engaged in a heated conversation in French as they braided a customer's hair. The customer alternately watched daytime talk shows and talked on her cell phone. This customer later confided to me:

> I don't know what they're talking about. It doesn't matter. They just talk and I watch TV until they're done. They don't speak English anyway. Tasha does a good job, so that's why I come here, but that's about it.

This customer's comments sharply contrast the statements from customers in salons owned by black American women. Customers in those shops expressed appreciation for the friendly interactions between all members of the salon community and spoke warmly of the camaraderie of the shop. Recall Lana's client's comment that coming to the salon was like "coming to a psychiatrist's office [where] we share everything." Such sentiments did not seem to be the case at salons owned by black ethnic women.

Summary

The experiences of black ethnic women provide important insights into the contours of the racial enclave economy. Race is frequently depicted as a monolithic category, despite research which suggests that within racial groups (such as Latino, Asian, and black), ethnic differences can facilitate contrasting viewpoints, experiences, and outcomes.[16] The experiences of black ethnic women in the racial enclave economy emphasize the reality that ethnic identity can differently construct black women's entrepreneurship (and paid work) within the enclave.

For black ethnic women, some aspects of their entrepreneurial experiences parallel those of other ethnic groups. The reliance on co-ethnic labor and the importance of kin networks in establishing entrepreneurship echo middleman minority and ethnic enclave patterns of entrepreneurship, respectively. These aspects of black ethnic women's entrepreneurship appear to be shaped by ethnicity, in the sense that the support of co-ethnics and kin appear to be part of ethnic entrepreneurship, regardless of racial classification. Further, middleman minority business owners are likely to experience strained relationships between themselves and members of the host society.[17] As such, the tension between black ethnic entrepreneurs and their customers conforms to established paradigms of ethnic entrepreneurship.

Yet while black ethnic women's entrepreneurship in some ways reflects the experiences of other immigrant entrepreneurs, their entrepreneurial experiences are, in important ways, shaped by systemic gendered racism. This creates similarities between their entrepreneurial work and black American women's. Gendered racism in occupational sectors and in the labor market reduces black ethnic women's access to economic stability. As with black American women, this makes entrepreneurship an attractive option. Yet gendered racism in the workplace that labels braided hairstyles unprofessional serves to thin out the available market. Ultimately, for black ethnic women, gendered racism is systemic and shapes their labor market and educational opportunities. As with black American women, this has an impact on their entrepreneurial experiences by creating a supply of potential entrepreneurs, even as there are constraints on the demand for the service they provide. Black ethnic women's entrepreneurship thus shows a different side of the racial enclave economy, one that is affected by systemic gendered racism but in several ways still conforms to established patterns of ethnic entrepreneurship.

The experiences of black ethnic women show that systemic gendered racism impacts black women's entrepreneurial activity in the racial enclave economy, even when black women claim different ethnic identities. Black ethnic women's experiences in the racial enclave economy are not identical to black American women's. However, there are important similarities, which suggest that systemic gendered racism affects racial minority women regardless of their ethnic identity.

CHAPTER SEVEN

Conclusion

See, if you own something, you have a vital stake in the future of America. This administration promotes what I call the ownership society. When people tell me statistics, they say, more people are owning their own small businesses, and a lot of minorities are owning their own small businesses. That's really good news for the future of the country. It also happens to be really good news for the economy. The more small businesses there are, the more likely it is people are going to find work.

—George Bush, Remarks to 2004 National Urban League Conference

While touted by President Bush and his administration as a surefire pathway to economic improvement, entrepreneurship is rarely considered in light of the pervasive structural inequalities that are embedded in American society. This book situates minority entrepreneurship in the context of systemic gendered racism that constructs ideologies, employs frames and counterframes, and shapes social institutions like the labor market, family, media, and the workplace. Gendered racism in these contexts impacts black women's entrepreneurship as salon owners in a multitude of ways, from the business decisions these women make, to issues of financing, to how they relate to and interact with their employees. These business ventures are shaped by gendered racism on several important fronts, demonstrating that as racial enclave economies, they are a significant, if understudied, component of minority entrepreneurship.

The initial conceptualization of gendered racism explores how black women's and men's experiences with racism were simultaneously shaped by gender. Essed speaks in particular of the stereotypes that black men are absent fathers, and that black women are sexually available.[1] Both are racist images that are specifically gendered. Other researchers have discussed the ways gendered racism produces controlling images that justify the mistreatment of racial minority men and women through public policy and in the workplace.[2] This work conceptualizes gendered racism primarily in terms of the images it produces and the ways these images facilitate minorities' unequal treatment.

The experiences of black women entrepreneurs suggest that gendered racism is not just limited to images. Rather, gendered racism is also systemic, embedded in numerous social institutions, and legitimized by ideologies. Gendered racism thus shapes institutions in social, economic, and political spheres. It is perpetuated through the media, economic institutions, workplaces, and in everyday interactions, thus functioning as a systemic phenomenon. The systemic nature of gendered racism means that it is promoted through ideology, frames, and controlling images. It is also contested through counterframes that seek to undermine its destructive messages.

Black women's entrepreneurial experiences show that controlling images are just one component of gendered racism. Gendered racist images like the modern Mammy, the criminal, the Jezebel, and the thug that are used to control blacks are powerful and problematic. However, these images coexist with gendered racist ideology that pits black women against each other as competitors in social and workplace environments. These images are also part of gendered racism in the labor market that channels black women into low-wage jobs. Furthermore, these images sanction gendered racist frames that depict black women as ghetto or too "hip-hop" and therefore as women who will devalue certain work environments. By considering the ways gendered racism shapes black women's entrepreneurship, it becomes clear that the presence of gendered racism in numerous arenas is a structural, systemic problem. The fact that systemic gendered racism informs black women's entrepreneurship and facilitates their construction of a racial enclave economy is indicative of how entrenched gendered racism is in the structure of American social systems.

Though I have documented black women's hair salons as examples of racial enclave economies, these economies likely exist in other, unstudied forms in the entrepreneurial landscape. As mentioned in the introduction, many professional black women are leaving paid employment to pursue entrepreneurship. Often, these women have college and/or advanced degrees and work in corporate spheres but found that the glass ceilings of corporate America effectively pushed them into entrepreneurship. Specifically, they grew tired of coping with racist and sexist corporate cultures and sought entrepreneurship as an alternate source of both income and personal satisfaction. Further research should address whether these women's entrepreneurial ventures also display characteristics of racial enclave economies. The assertion that institutionalized racism and sexism in the workplace is a factor in pursuing entrepreneurship suggests that their entrepreneurial ventures may in fact be examples of racial enclave economies.

Future studies should also consider the impact of systemic gendered racism on the entrepreneurial activities of other racial groups. The tendency in the ethnic entrepreneurship literature has been to focus on ethnic groups, particularly ethnic men, without considering the ways ethnicity exists in a racial context. Consequently, we know about the entrepreneurial experiences of Cubans but are less familiar with the ways systemic gendered racism shapes entrepreneurship among a broad group of Latino/as—Dominicans, Puerto Ricans, Mexicans, or Nicaraguans. Placing ethnic groups' entrepreneurial experiences in the context of the very real and well-documented racial discrimination of U.S. society offers a different picture of minority entrepreneurship—one that is missing from much of the existing research.

Considering the ways that systemic gendered racism shapes other groups' entrepreneurship will likely reveal a different picture than that of the black women business owners interviewed here. Systemic gendered racism does not produce identical or interchangeable experiences for various racial groups. The experiences of working-class black women may have some similarities to those of working class Latinas, but they will not be synonymous because race/gender groups exist on different levels in a racial, gendered hierarchy. Sociologist Eduardo Bonilla-Silva has argued that the United States is moving toward a racial structure that resembles Latin American countries wherein Asians and lighter skinned Latinos become "honorary whites."[3] While other research contradicts this claim and suggests that in no way do whites consider these racial minorities to be honorary whites, these studies do suggest a hierarchical ranking wherein certain minorities are construed as more appealing than others.[4]

This ranking system may shape various race/gender groups' paths to entrepreneurship, the types of businesses they open, and their economic success. Whites, an important market for any minority entrepreneurs, may feel more comfortable patronizing business ventures owned by Latino men than by black men, particularly if these businesses involve interpersonal interaction with the owners and these owners are lighter-skinned Latinos. Similarly, systemic gendered racism in the economic, media, and political sectors may concentrate Asian American women entrepreneurs in personal service industries but they may be situated in areas (nail services, for example) where they have more access to white customers than do black women entrepreneurs. Future work should consider variations in racial enclave economies across racial lines.

Comparisons to Ethnic Economies

In several ways, the consequences and successes of racial enclave economy businesses like the hair salon are contradictory. Black women's hair salons, for example, employ a counterframe to systemic gendered racism when they purposely establish their salons as safe spaces for black women. However, by seeking out and relying on a clientele predominantly comprised of black women, they reproduce the racial and gendered segregation of the larger society. Unfortunately, gender and racial segregation usually works to black women's disadvantage. The effects of this counterframe are therefore mixed, as owners require a racially homogenous environment in order to provide social support. However, this limited clientele establishes boundaries on owners' earning capacity. Hence, while the owners can counter systemic gendered racism by supporting black women, they also reproduce segregation that curtails their profits.

Though salon ownership enables black women to experience socioeconomic advancement through increases in income and wealth, they still experience ghettoization in that they establish businesses in personal service industries. Businesses in this industry tend to be the lowest-paying and least prestigious areas of minority entrepreneurship.[5] Thus, even as salon owners are engaging in entrepreneurial activity that allows them to increase their economic position, this increase is still minor relative to other, nontraditional areas of minority entrepreneurship like construction or manufacturing. These contradictory outcomes suggest that like other forms of entrepreneurship, businesses in the racial enclave economy have their strengths and weaknesses. These businesses manage to carve an economically successful niche despite systemic gendered racism, but ultimately are still bound by its constraints.

In these ways, racial enclave economies maintain some parallels to the forms of ethnic entrepreneurship that are so frequently the subject of sociological research. As others have pointed out, businesses in the ethnic economy rarely compete with mainstream businesses in terms of revenue or production.[6] Black women's hair salons in the racial enclave economy are no exception. While they do provide occupational opportunity and the possibility for economic improvement to black women, like ethnic economies, they generally do not compete financially with mainstream businesses. Additional research would be necessary, however, to assess whether these salons earn revenues that are comparable to white-owned salons.

Like ethnic economies, salons are an example of racial enclave establishments that also rely heavily on solidarity, particularly for black ethnic women. However, solidarity in the racial enclave economy does not exactly mirror the solidarity in ethnic economies. Researchers argue that ethnic solidarity helps co-ethnics find work in ethnic economies, particularly through weak ties.[7] While ethnic solidarity is very valuable for black ethnic women seeking employment in hair salons, for black American salon owners, this solidarity is more precise. These owners rarely articulated their business decisions and actions as a function of racial solidarity, but characterized their work as specifically intended to help black *women*. It is not just racial solidarity, but racial and gendered solidarity, that is present in these businesses in the racial enclave economy. One does not take precedence over the other.

Similarities between racial enclave economies and ethnic economies do exist. Yet, it is important to underscore that the key difference between these forms of minority entrepreneurship is the important role systemic gendered racism plays in shaping racial enclave economies. The parallels between the two forms of entrepreneurship, specifically concerning financial profits and the role of solidarity, should not mask the reality that systemic gendered racism creates entrepreneurial experiences that must be explicitly addressed. Racial enclave economies thus differ from ethnic economies because of the central role systemic gendered racism plays on entrepreneurial decisions, motivations, and actions.

Current Policy toward Minority Entrepreneurs

With a clearer understanding of the existence, contours, and contradictions of the racial enclave economy, policies about entrepreneurship—particularly minority entrepreneurship—beg further examination. The Bush administration's current policy toward minority entrepreneurship is extremely encouraging and supportive. As stated in the opening quote for this chapter, the current administration describes entrepreneurship as a crucial cornerstone of economic stability. Yet the Bush administration paints entrepreneurship in very broad terms, without considering the underlying distinctions that can differently shape business ownership among minority groups. Without this more nuanced view, this administration supports policies that may not be as applicable or helpful to minority women entrepreneurs, in general, or to entrepreneurs in the racial enclave economy, in particular.

Current administrative policies include several initiatives designed to support minority entrepreneurship. The Bush administration has partnered with the Urban League and has committed federal funding to implementing "one-stop centers." These centers are designed to help minority entrepreneurs learn important strategies and specific information about engaging in entrepreneurship. In addition, the administration also boasts that loans to minorities through the Small Business Administration (SBA) continued to exceed the loan rates of years past; and that through processes of contract unbundling and procurement initiatives, minorities now have greater access to federal contracts. Finally, the administration seeks to bolster minority entrepreneurship through increased funding to the Minority Business Development Agency (MBDA) and through the African Growth and Opportunity Acceleration Act of 2004, which encourages export opportunities and business linkages with African countries. In this section, I examine the effectiveness of each of these policies in light of the experiences of black women entrepreneurs in the racial enclave economy.

One-Stop Centers

On a superficial level, one-stop centers are a useful strategy in promoting minority entrepreneurship. These centers are intended to provide comprehensive training to minorities interested in business ownership, including information on generating economic capital and developing and maintaining important business contacts. Federal government initiatives to promote minority entrepreneurship are laudable, but one-stop centers ignore the realities of how information is distributed in the racial enclave economy. Among women hair salon owners, this information is quite effectively disseminated through interactions between owners and employees. Thus, it is worth asking whether minority women in the racial enclave economy would utilize one-stop centers, given that in the case of the hair salon, they are able to access important information through social networks that are established and maintained through the business.

One-stop centers are also limited in their ability to address the issues black women entrepreneurs cited with regard to securing funding. None of the salon owners interviewed for this study were able to access funding from traditional sources. Instead, all relied on personal savings or loans from family and friends. This is unsurprising given biases in the financial industry that confer loans to minority men and all women at lower rates than white men.[8] Though one-stop centers are intended to offer information to potential entrepreneurs—including possible sources of funding—this information does not guarantee that black women in the racial enclave will be able to avail themselves of start-up capital from these sources.

One-stop centers could conceivably address owners' complaints that they were often hindered by a lack of knowledge about investment opportunities. In chapter 3, I argued that unfamiliarity with investment options has a particular impact on black women due to the implications for childrearing and the economic stability of families. One-stop centers could be useful were they to offer information about investment and financial planning to potential entrepreneurs in the racial enclave economy. While many women sought to pass on recently gained knowledge about investment and financial planning to their stylists, these same owners often regretted that they had not been privy to such knowledge at the onset of entrepreneurship. One-stop centers could be extremely beneficial to minority women in the racial enclave economy if they helped to reach women who were not taught strategies and the importance of sound financial planning and investment.

Finally, the results of this study suggest that one-stop centers would do well to aggressively reach out to entrepreneurs rather than waiting for potential business owners to visit them. Given that these women felt a degree of confidence in launching their businesses since, as they put it, "Black women will go get their hair done," several did not feel a need to do a great deal of in-depth research prior to opening their salons. Recall that all of the respondents had worked as stylists in another black woman-owned salon before becoming entrepreneurs, and gained valuable preparation for business ownership from this work experience. Consequently, one-stop centers could conceivably maximize their effectiveness if they actively sought out minority entrepreneurs in the racial enclave, as these business owners may feel sufficiently prepared for entrepreneurship that they do not avail themselves of these centers.

Small Business Administration Loans

The current administration cites evidence of its support for minority entrepreneurship by boasting that the rates of loans to minority entrepreneurs from the Small Business Administration (SBA) continue to exceed previous years' rates. Once again, this claim rings hollow when racial enclave economies are taken into consideration. As discussed, none of the women interviewed for this study was able to secure a loan from the SBA or other traditional financing sources. Hence, to cite increased SBA loans to minorities does not necessarily suggest that these loans are going to entrepreneurs in the racial enclave economy whose businesses are largely impacted by systemic gendered racism.

The discrepancy between the government's claims of increased SBA loans and respondents' realities of relying on nontraditional funding may be attributed to several factors. Some women interviewed for this study may not have tried to get loans through the SBA. Other women may have tried and not had sufficient credit or income to be attractive candidates for a loan. There is also the possibility that the SBA itself may also be constrained by the same issues of systemic gendered racism that impact other lending institutions—issues that play a role in increasing the difficulties that minority men and all women face in gaining access to economic capital. This would suggest that SBA loans to minority entrepreneurs could increase, while working-class black women entrepreneurs would still have a difficult time accessing funding. At any rate, given the experiences of the women interviewed for this study, more SBA loans to minorities does not necessarily indicate that a broad range of minority entrepreneurs have access to or are utilizing this source of funding.

Increased Minority Access to Federal Contracts

Administrative efforts to unbundle contracts and support procurement initiatives deserve credit for recognizing how these processes can adversely affect minority entrepreneurs. Bundling contracts involves pulling contracts together so that companies can bid on a group of contracts rather than individual ones; unbundling keeps contracts separate. Procurement initiatives are efforts to increase access to gaining these contracts. Together, these policies allow contracts to be bid upon individually, thus increasing the ability of minority entrepreneurs to bid on contracts to do work for the federal government. Ultimately, these policies are intended to bolster minority entrepreneurs' access to federal contracts and the economic gain that a successful bid includes.

These policies may in fact be useful for large companies in nontraditional areas of black entrepreneurship, like construction and manufacturing. If, through contract unbundling, a black-owned construction company gets a contract to build a new government office building, this is indeed a coup. If procurement initiatives enable a black-owned manufacturing company to make the furniture exclusively used in government buildings, this too is an enormous achievement. These policies, however, are virtually irrelevant to black-women-owned businesses in the racial enclave economy like the hair salon. Salon owners like Tanisha and Greta, though extremely successful among the sample, will not bid on a contract to be the exclusive hair stylists for government officials.

This is not to suggest that contract unbundling and procurement initiatives have no value. Clearly, to the extent that they benefit minority-owned companies, they are important. However, it is worth pointing out that these policies will benefit entrepreneurs who own businesses in areas where blacks are still underrepresented.[9] It is also important to note that while systemic gendered racism channels black women into particular areas of entrepreneurship, these areas do not benefit from the contract unbundling and procurement initiatives of which the current administration is so proud.

Minority Business Development Agency

The Minority Business Development Agency (MBDA) is a federally funded agency situated in the U.S. Department of Commerce. The official mandate of the MBDA is to "achieve entrepreneurial parity for minority business enterprises by actively promoting their ability to grow and compete in the global economy."[10] The MBDA achieves this by offering support for "medium to large businesses enterprises that can have a significant impact on employment and the tax base in their communities."[11] Federal support for this agency is thus designed to promote larger minority-owned businesses that can create economic stability and boost employment in minority communities.

As with contract unbundling and procurement initiatives, funding for the MBDA is well intentioned and ostensibly designed to benefit minority entrepreneurs. Yet when racial enclave economies are taken into consideration, the MBDA's effectiveness is limited. As the MBDA is constructed to offer financial support for large minority-owned businesses, entrepreneurs in racial enclave economies like salon owners will be easily overlooked. Though these businesses are by no means large-scale enterprises that employ vast numbers of minorities, these entrepreneurial ventures offer working-class black women one of few viable opportunities for economic stability and socioeconomic advancement, as owners or as employees. The opportunities and benefits that salon ownership provides, however, are disregarded when federal organizations concentrate their energies on larger minority business enterprises. Like contract unbundling and procurement initiatives, these efforts to support minority entrepreneurship are perhaps most beneficial to minorities in large-scale, nontraditional forms of entrepreneurship rather than the smaller-scale hair salons owned by some black women in the racial enclave economy.

African Growth and Opportunity Acceleration Act

The African Growth and Opportunity Act (AGOA) was recently extended to 2015, becoming the African Growth and Opportunity Acceleration Act. This act is designed to encourage and increase minority business exports and trade with African countries. Supported by the MBDA and SBA, this act promotes trade between the United States and many poor nations in sub-Saharan Africa.[12] Coming on the heels of renewed attention to devastating poverty on the African continent and a 2005 decision by G8 countries to enact debt forgiveness for several African countries, AGOA represents the continued effort on behalf of developed nations and world financial bodies to encourage development and economic stability in Africa.

The AGOA's emphasis is on promoting trade between the United States and African nations. In fact, one company that has already benefited from AGOA policies is the U.S. clothing company Brandot LLC. As of 2004, Brandot LLC opened several factories in Madagascar that produce clothing for stores including Gap, Abercrombie and Fitch, Express, and Liz Claiborne.[13] Additional factories are planned for Ghana and Uganda and call centers are being considered for these countries, as well.

As currently instituted, the AGOA appears to implement free-trade policies that include African workers in the global workforce of employees who do not enjoy safe working conditions, insurance, access to sufficient food, water, health care, or even a living wage.[14] These policies are criticized for promoting *free trade* rather than *fair trade*—a trade system that better enables workers to combat the crushing poverty they are likely to face in developing nations. Rather than enabling or encouraging entrepreneurs on the African continent to compete with large multinational corporations, these policies enable already wealthy corporations to multiply their profits by employing Africans for minimal wages.

Since the current administration often emphasizes the AGOA as part of its initiatives to promote minority entrepreneurship, it is worth considering how AGOA policies may impact black ethnic women within the (American) racial enclave economy. The AGOA may have the potential to facilitate black ethnic women's participation in the racial enclave economy by exacerbating the economic constraints that exist in many African nations and make work in America appealing by comparison. It is impossible to suggest how—or if at all—the AGOA can affect women's immigration to the United States. However, given that with free trade policies, women often are channeled into dehumanizing jobs that do not pay a living wage and adversely affect children and families, AGOA policies may in fact contribute to the ways black ethnic women are affected by systemic gendered racism, thereby shaping their work in the racial enclave economy.

Upon close examination, it becomes evident that without taking into consideration the realities of racial enclave economies and the role of systemic gendered racism in creating these enclaves, current policies may be less effective than anticipated in encouraging minority entrepreneurship. These policies are grounded in assumptions that ignore the reality of systemic gendered racism and the consequent emergence of racial enclave economies.

Further, entrepreneurship policies are so broadly designed that they are unable to make critical distinctions between racial and ethnic minorities and how their experiences vary in ways that shape their entrepreneurial activity. Current policy efforts also fail to take into consideration the complexities of minority entrepreneurship, assuming a one-size-fits-all orientation that imperfectly addresses the diverse experiences of racial minority groups.

Potential Policies for Racial Enclave Economies

The aforementioned policies are written with broad strokes, and do not take the complexities of racial enclave economies into consideration. So what policies would better serve racial minority entrepreneurs in the racial enclave economy? On a small scale, policy initiatives that assist black women entrepreneurs in wealth creation and development would address the primary complaint these women raised about their work as business owners: that they often learn too late how translate their incomes into wealth and therefore maximize their earnings from the salon. Public policy that seeks to inform historically (and currently) disadvantaged populations about how to generate wealth would benefit these women by supporting their efforts to gain economic stability. Such a policy might involve restructuring one-stop centers so that they aggressively seek out entrepreneurs and offer information about creating wealth, or funding community centers that provide financial planning services in low- and middle-income areas.

Additionally, public policy that increases black women entrepreneurs' access to economic capital and funding sources would also enable these women to pursue business ownership more competitively. Women interviewed for this study revealed a general reliance on nontraditional funding sources, in part because they had difficulty accessing mainstream funding sources like banks and governmental financial assistance. Although federal funds exist that are explicitly designed to facilitate minority entrepreneurship, these women either were unable to utilize these funds or were unaware of them. Rather than simply earmarking these funds, federal and state policy could include proactive efforts to match these monies to prospective entrepreneurs.

These policies would offer black women easier access to start-up capital and facilitate their wealth-building enterprise. However, these policies are only effective on a small scale. Ultimately, these types of policies do nothing to destabilize the larger social processes of systemic gendered racism that minimize black women's access to wealth in the first place. The results of this study indicate that black women who are hair salon owners have been able to capitalize on some of the negative ideological, economic, and social aspects of systemic gendered racism in order to create business establishments that challenged these tenets and offered financial stability. Yet they still reproduce aspects of gendered racism within these establishments. As such, even though these women have, to an extent, been able to exploit systemic gendered racism to their economic advantage, I argue that eliminating systemic gendered racism as a whole is the most efficacious pathway to economic stability for black women.

This book documents ways that systemic gendered racism has played a role in black women's entrepreneurial activity and argues that this phenomenon is a significant factor in the creation of the racial enclave economy. However, this should not obscure the fact that systemic gendered racism helps to constrain black women's labor market opportunities, thus making entrepreneurship in the racial enclave economy a relatively more attractive option. Nor should we ignore the fact that the ideological messages of systemic gendered racism—which emphasize black women's physical and social undesirability— can be replicated in businesses in the racial enclave economy. Elimination of systemic gendered racism may well drastically alter the construction of the racial enclave economy. It is worth considering, though, whether the absence of systemic gendered racism might restructure the racial enclave economy in more positive ways.

Consider, for example, economic policies that might rectify the pervasive influence of systemic gendered racism in society. In their study of institutionalized racism in various settings, Brown et al. suggest policy changes in the form of "more investment in job training and creation, early childhood education, [and] accessible health care for all."[15] These changes would arguably affect the working-class black women here by offering more work opportunities than the ones to which systemic gendered racism limits them; making child care available in other ways besides having to establish a business and set one's own schedule; and establishing a health care system that does not disproportionately penalize the poor and working class. The implementation of these policies might change the current structure of the racial enclave economy, but they would do so by providing more choices, options, and stability for working-class black women.

Feminist researchers have also drawn important attention to the continued existence of sex segregation in labor markets.[16] They argue that the eradication of occupational sex segregation would have enormous impact in closing wage gaps between women and men. This policy would also work to undermine systemic gendered racism in society by disabling the channels that push women into "women's" occupations, which almost universally offer lower pay and prestige than "men's" work.[17] Challenging systemic gendered racism in this way helps to increase working-class black women's access to jobs that may be better paying (therefore offering more economic stability) than the low-wage women's jobs that provide the alternative to work in the racial enclave economy. Undoing this process might minimize women's entrepreneurial activity in the racial enclave economy, but again, the change to the structure of the enclave comes with more opportunity.

Finally, it is imperative that the ideological components of systemic gendered racism—which emphasize a racially specific beauty myth and/or suggest that working-class blacks are "ghetto"—be destroyed. The results of this work show that these aspects of systemic gendered racism are especially dangerous given the ease with which they are reproduced by blacks in spaces that, paradoxically, are designed to counteract these very ideological messages. Few researchers that espouse policy changes that might undermine aspects of systemic gendered racism also discuss how to eliminate the ideological underpinnings of inequality, possibly because such ideologies are so insidious and omnipresent. One hope is that the implementation of the aforementioned policies will destroy the ideological components of systemic gendered racism along with its structural and economic aspects. This may well work. Bonilla-Silva convincingly argues that social, political, and economic changes have altered the underlying racial ideology that pervades American social systems, although Feagin effectively documents the ways in which this ideology has remained disturbingly constant over time.[18] If Feagin is correct, then broader policy solutions are needed to correct the deep-rooted ideological aspects of systemic gendered racism that are reproduced even in racial enclave economies.

Ultimately, the point of this book has been to demonstrate how systemic gendered racism influences the entrepreneurial patterns and practices of minority women to create a racial enclave economy. Like all other forms of paid work, self-employment, and entrepreneurship, the racial enclave economy has its strengths and weaknesses. However, it is important first and foremost to recognize the existence of this form of entrepreneurship, rather than continuing to relegate black women's business ownership to preexisting but ill-fitting paradigms of minority business ownership, or ignoring the specific contours of this form of entrepreneurship. Hopefully, this work will motivate others to continue the exploration of racial enclave economies and to consider the far-reaching implications of systemic gendered racism in the arenas of paid work and entrepreneurship.

Appendix: Methodology
Methods of Data Collection

I rely on in-depth interviews with twenty-three black women salon owners to make the case for black hair salons as an example of a racial enclave economy. In the interviews, the women discussed their work history, the factors that led them to the hair industry, and the motivators that compelled them to become entrepreneurs. They talked about the struggles and specific challenges they faced as entrepreneurs in this field, and the particular advantages and drawbacks of work in this area. Respondents also discussed sources of competition in the field and their long- and short-term goals as entrepreneurs.

Eleven shops were located in the more urban part of a major metropolitan city and the other twelve were located in the suburban county adjacent to this city. The shops also provided different services—eleven women-owned shops worked with both chemically straightened hair and nonprocessed hair; seven women-owned shops worked exclusively with chemically straightened hair; and five women-owned shops provided braiding services or worked exclusively with women with natural hair that had not been chemically treated.

Of the women interviewed, eight were married, one was engaged, and one was divorced. The remainder had never married. Eleven women were mothers, and of these eleven, four had children older than 18. The children of the remaining seven women ranged in age from 1 to 16. The women interviewed also ranged in age, with five women (all owners) under the age of 30. The oldest owner interviewed was in her fifties, the youngest was 25.

The locations of the salons covered a wide range, including working-class neighborhoods, middle-class areas on the outskirts of the city, and urban, lower-class neighborhoods. Similarly, clienteles ranged in income but did not vary widely with regard to race and gender. Some owners had a handful of white or Asian customers but, at each shop, the majority of the clientele were black women. The location of the shop tended to mirror the social class of the clientele, for example, shops in middle-class neighborhoods usually had mostly middle-class women as a customer base.

Of the twenty-three owners interviewed, all started as stylists prior to branching off to own their own salons. In fact, some of the owners interviewed here had previously employed women when they were still working as stylists, before they became owners. Additionally, all owners also styled hair in their salons and maintained a regular clientele. Owners estimated that they contributed forty- to sixty-hour workweeks in their salons.

Salon owners interviewed for this study typically hired one to three stylists to work in their shops. Two owners worked alone, and on the other end of the spectrum, one owner employed fourteen stylists, which was more than any other owner interviewed for this study. All the owners operated salons in which they charged stylists booth rent. Under this system, stylists pay a monthly rent to owners for the use of space at the salon. Stylists are then permitted to keep all money from business transactions but are not guaranteed any benefits like medical insurance, dental insurance, retirement plans, or sick leave. Though stylists are technically independent contractors, they must follow the rules and guidelines established by the salon owner, and either party can terminate the working relationship.

All of the owners interviewed here hailed from working-class backgrounds. Though scholars continue to debate the best way to identify and measure social class, I considered education, income, and wealth as interrelated factors that determine one's position in the class hierarchy. As members of the working class, these women had been previously employed as sales associates, fast-food workers, or telemarketers, positions that generated annual incomes of about $25,000 or less annually. They did not own their homes, although six had owned cars, and none had amassed any other forms of wealth or educational attainment past high school (though all owners completed cosmetology school). Furthermore, none of these women were raised in families where the combined household incomes reached the middle-class or upper middle-class levels of $40,000 to $75,000 per year.

I used the extended case study method to analyze the data from these interviews. The extended case study method, as developed by Burawoy, "seeks generalization through reconstructing existing generalizations."[1] Put another way, the extended case study method relies on existing theory to produce new theory to be applied. This differs from grounded theory, another widely used method of analyzing qualitative data, because it emphasizes the creation of new theory to fit and describe the phenomenon being studied as aptly as possible.

There were several advantages to using the extended case study method. First, as I have described in earlier chapters, sociological study of black entrepreneurs is rather scarce. Because most researchers fail to note the distinction between race and ethnicity, most studies either ignore black entrepreneurship or attempt to explain why it does not follow the trends of ethnic groups. Studies of black women entrepreneurs are even more scarce, given that most researchers in this area consider women's participation in entrepreneurship as incidental or peripheral, but usually fail to consider the experiences of women entrepreneurs directly.[2] As such, a method of analysis that facilitates the development of new theory is especially prescient for an area of study that is generally overlooked in the literature.

Secondly, though the literature on black women entrepreneurs is scant, the extended case study method has been successfully used in prior research examining black women in beauty salons. Kim Battle-Waters's study *Sheila's Shop* explores how black working-class women construct a sense of racial and gender victorization from their interactions at a black beauty salon.[3] Using the extended case study method, Battle-Waters concludes that existing theories intended to explain the experiences of minority women do not fully take into consideration all the nuances of the interplay between race, gender, and class that are salient to working-class black women. Her reliance on the extended case study method leads her to develop the concept of racial and gender victorization to convey the "strength, optimism, and self-determinism" these women expressed.[4]

Given that there is so little research exploring the subject matter of this book, and that one of the few studies that addresses similar topics successfully used this method, the extended case study method was deemed the best technique for analyzing the data generated from this study. My expectation was that this method would enable me to identify the emergent and new theoretical concepts inherent in the data.

Notes

Foreword

1. Thomas Jefferson, *Notes on the State of Virginia*, ed. Frank Shuffelton (New York: Penguin Books, 1999 [1785]), p. 145.

2. Joe R. Feagin, *Systemic Racism: A Theory of Oppression* (New York: Routledge, 2006), pp. 25–28.

Introduction

1. Respondents' names and identifying details have been changed to protect their anonymity.

2. T. Shawn Taylor, "Wall Street and Business Wednesdays: Self-Styled Entrepreneurs: Salon Ownership Affords African American Women a Comfortable Living." http://www.blackelectorate.com/articles.asp?ID=1348, posted April 13, 2005, accessed May 15, 2007.

3. Center for Women's Business Research, *Businesses Owned by African American Women in the United States, 2006: A Fact Sheet* (Washington, DC: Center for Women's Business Research, 2006).

4. Jim Hopkins, "African American Women Step up in Business World," *USA Today*, August 24, 2006.

Chapter 1: Introducing the Racial Enclave Economy

1. Sucheng Chan, *Hmong Means Free: Life in Laos and America* (Philadelphia: Temple University Press, 1994); Yen Le Espiritu, *Asian American Women and Men:*

Labor, Laws and Love (Thousand Oaks, CA: Sage, 1997); and Stacey Lee, *Unraveling the Model Minority Stereotype* (New York: Teachers College Press, 1996).

2. Lee, *Unraveling.*

3. Michael Omi and Howard Winant, *Racial Formation in the United States from the 1960s to the 1980s* (New York: Routledge, 1986).

4. Eduardo Bonilla-Silva, *White Supremacy and Racism in the Post–Civil Rights Era* (Boulder, CO: Lynne Rienner Publishers, 2001).

5. Joe Feagin, *Systemic Racism: A Theory of Oppression* (New York: Routledge, 2006).

6. Feagin, *Systemic Racism*, 7.

7. Angela Davis, *Women, Race, and Class* (New York: Random House, 1981).

8. Juliet Walker, *The History of Black Business in America: Capitalism, Race, Entrepreneurship* (New York: McMillan Library Reference, 1998).

9. Eric Foner, *Who Owns History?* (New York: Hill and Wang, 2002).

10. Feagin, *Systemic Racism*, 128.

11. Ellis Cose, *The Rage of a Privileged Class* (New York: HarperCollins, 1993); Marlene Durr and John R. Logan, "Racial Submarkets in Government Employment: African American Managers in New York State," *Sociological Forum* 12, no. 3 (1997): 353–70; Joe Feagin and Melvin Sikes, *Living with Racism: The Black Middle Class Experience* (Boston: Beacon Press, 1994); Joleen Kirschenmen and Kathryn M. Neckerman, "'We'd Love to Hire Them But . . .' The Meaning of Race for Employers," in *Rethinking the Color Line: Readings in Race and Ethicity*, ed. Charles A. Gallagher (New York: McGraw-Hill, 2006), 306–17; Jennifer L. Pierce, *Gender Trials: Emotional Lives in Contemporary Law Firms* (Berkeley: University of California Press, 1995). Mary Thierry, "Who Protects and Serves Me?" *Gender and Society* 16, no. 4 (2002): 524–45.

12. Feagin and Sikes, *Living with Racism.*

13. Michael K. Brown, Martin Carnoy, Elliott Currie, Troy Duster, David B. Oppenheimer, Marjorie B. Schultz, and David Wellman, *Whitewashing Race: The Myth of a Color-Blind Society* (Berkeley: University of California Press, 2003); Thomas M. Shapiro, *The Hidden Costs of Being African American: How Wealth Perpetuates Inequality* (New York: Oxford University Press, 2004).

14. Though I attribute the idea of blacks as inherently inferior to whites as part of an earlier white racist frame, it is important to point out that this ideology has by no means completely disappeared. As recently as 1994, Richard Herrnstein and Charles Murray's widely discussed book *The Bell Curve* revisited the themes of black genetic inferiority as a rationale for eliminating funding for various social service programs. While many sociologists and other researchers exposed the flawed reasoning and statistical manipulations that were made in the book, its premise and conclusions received national attention and were credited with affecting national public policy, especially welfare reform.

15. Feagin, *Systemic Racism*, 306.

16. Joe Feagin, *Racist America* (New York: Routledge, 2000), and Feagin, *Systemic Racism.*

17. Feagin, *Systemic Racism*.

18. Feagin, *Systemic Racism*, 74.

19. Johnetta B. Cole and Beverly Guy-Sheftall, *Gender Talk: The Struggle for Women's Equality in African American Communities* (New York: One World/Ballantine, 2003); Patricia Hill Collins, *Black Sexual Politics: African Americans, Gender, and the New Racism* (New York: Routledge, 2004); Bonnie T. Dill, *Across the Boundaries of Race and Class: An Exploration of Work and Family Among Black Female Domestic Servants* (New York: Routledge, 1993); Espiritu, *Asian American Women and Men*; bell hooks, *Feminist Theory: From Margin to Center*, second ed. (Cambridge, MA: South End Press, 2000); Deborah K. King, "Multiple Jeopardy, Multiple Consciousness: The Context of a Black Feminist Ideology," *Signs: Journal of Women in Culture and Society* 14, no. 1 (1988): 42–72.

20. Philomena Essed, *Understanding Everyday Racism* (Newbury Park, CA: Sage, 1991), 31.

21. Essed, *Understanding Everyday Racism*; Judith Lorber, "Night to His Day: The Social Construction of Gender," in *Men and Masculinity*, ed. Theodore F. Cohen (Belmont, CA: Wadsworth, 2001), 19–28; Candace West and Don Zimmerman, "Doing Gender," *Gender & Society* 1 (1987): 125–51.

22. Kim Lersch and Joe Feagin, "Violent Police-Citizen Encounters: An Analysis of Major Newspaper Accounts," *Critical Sociology* 22 (1996): 29–49.

23. Patricia Hill Collins, *Black Feminist Thought* (New York: Routledge, 1990); Collins, *Black Feminist Thought*, second ed. (New York: Routledge, 2000).

24. See Joe Feagin, Hernan Vera, and Nikitah Imani, *The Agony of Education: Black Students at White Colleges and Universities* (New York: Routledge, 1996); and Ann Arnett Ferguson, *Bad Boys: Public Schools in the Making of Black Masculinity* (Ann Arbor: University of Michigan Press, 2000).

25. Ferguson, *Bad Boys*.

26. Ferguson, *Bad Boys*, 85.

27. Collins, *Black Sexual Politics*.

28. Espiritu, *Asian American Women and Men*.

29. Collins, *Black Feminist Thought*; Collins, *Black Sexual Politics*; and Espiritu, *Asian American Women and Men*.

30. Ferguson, *Bad Boys*; Lee, *Unraveling*.

31. See Deborah Woo, "The Gap Between Striving and Achieving: The Case of Asian American Women," in *Race, Class, and Gender*, second ed., ed. Margaret Andersen and Patricia Hill Collins (Belmont, CA: Wadsworth Publishing, 1995), 218–26. Despite their overrepresentation in professional positions, Asian American women still experience wage disparity with Asian American men, who outearn them.

32. Hubert M. Blalock, *Toward a Theory of Minority-group Relations* (New York: Wiley, 1967).

33. Eunju Lee, *Gendered Processes: Korean Immigrant Small Business Ownership* (New York: LFB Scholarly Publishing, 2006), 13.

34. Yussef Simmonds, interview with Andrew Young in the *Los Angeles Sentinel*, August 12, 2006.

35. Edna Bonacich, "A Theory of Middleman Minorities," *American Sociological Review* 38, no. 5 (1973): 583–94.

36. Bonacich, "A Theory of Middleman Minorities."

37. Espiritu, *Asian American Women and Men.*

38. Walter P. Zenner, *Minorities in the Middle: A Cross-Cultural Analysis* (New York: SUNY Press, 1991).

39. Lee, *Gendered Processes*, 15.

40. Jimy M. Sanders and Victor Nee, "Limits of Ethnic Solidarity in the Enclave Economy," *American Sociological Review* 52, no. 6 (1987): 745–67.

41. Pyong Gap Min, *Caught in the Middle: Korean Merchants in America's Multi-Ethnic Cities* (Berkeley: University of California Press, 1996).

42. Alejandro Portes and Robert Bach, *Latin Journey: Cuban and Mexican Immigrants in the United States* (Berkeley: University of California Press, 1985).

43. Alejandro Portes and Leif Jensen, "The Enclave and the Entrants: Patterns of Ethnic Enterprise in Miami Before and After Mariel," *American Sociological Review* 54, no. 6 (1989): 929–49.

44. Portes and Bach, *Latin Journey.*

45. M. Patricia Fernandez-Kelly and Anna M. Garcia, "Power Surrendered, Power Restored: The Politics of Home and Work among Hispanic Women in Southern California and Southern Florida," in *Women, Politics and Change*, ed. Louise Tilly and Patricia Guerin (New York: Russell Sage Foundation, 1990), 130–49.

46. Bonacich, "A Theory of Middleman Minorities"; and Portes and Bach, *Latin Journey.*

47. Edna Bonacich and John Modell, *The Economic Basis of Solidarity: Small Business in the Japanese American Community* (Berkeley: University of California Press, 1980); Lee, *Gendered Processes*; Portes and Jensen, "The Enclave and the Entrants"; Min Zhou and John R. Logan, "Return on Human Capital in Ethnic Enclaves: New York City's Chinatown," *American Sociological Review* 54, no. 5 (1989): 809–20.

48. Alejandro Portes and Min Zhou, "Self-Employment and the Earnings of Immigrants," *American Sociological Review* 61, no. 2 (1996): 219–30.

49. Ivan H. Light and Steven J. Gold, *Ethnic Economies* (San Diego: Academic Press, 2000), 199.

50. Light and Gold, *Ethnic Economies*, 199.

51. Light and Gold, *Ethnic Economies*, 202.

52. Light and Gold, *Ethnic Economies*, 202.

53. Joe Feagin and Eileen O'Brien, *White Men on Race: Power, Privilege, and the Shaping of Cultural Consciousness* (Boston: Beacon Press, 2003); Brown et al., *Whitewashing Race*; and Shapiro, *The Hidden Costs of Being African American.*

54. E. Franklin Frazier, *Black Bourgeoisie: The Rise of a New Middle Class in the United States* (Glencoe, IL: The Free Press, 1957).

55. Bart Landry, *The New Black Middle Class* (Berkeley: University of California Press, 1987); and Earl Ofari Hutchinson, *The Myth of Black Capitalism* (New York: Monthly Review Press, 1970).

56. John S. Butler, *Entrepreneurship and Self-Help among Black Americans: A Reconsideration of Race and Economics*, second edition (New York: SUNY Press, 2005).

57. Butler, *Entrepreneurship*, 242.

58. Butler, *Entrepreneurship*, 242.

59. Walker, *The History of Black Business in America*.

60. Center for Women's Business Research, *African American Women-Owned Businesses in the United States, 2004: A Fact Sheet* (Washington, DC: Center for Women's Business Research, 2004).

61. Portes and Bach, *Latin Journey*; Portes and Jensen "The Enclave and the Entrants"; and Portes and Zhou, "Self-Employment."

62. Little is known specifically about Latinas' entrepreneurial activity; most research fails to take gender into consideration when exploring racial groups' entrepreneurship. However, beauty and hair services are currently a growing field for Latina business owners.

Chapter 2: History of Black Entrepreneurship

1. John S. Butler, *Entrepreneurship and Self-Help among Black Americans*, first edition (Albany, NY: SUNY Press, 1991).

2. Ivan H. Light, *Ethnic Enterprise in America* (Berkeley: University of California Press, 1972).

3. John S. Butler, *Entrepreneurship and Self-Help among Black Americans*, second edition (Albany, NY: SUNY Press, 2005).

4. Butler, *Entrepreneurship and Self-Help* (2005).

5. Albert Harris, "Political, Racial and Differential Psychology," *Journal of Social Psychology* 7 (1936): 474–79.

6. Butler, *Entrepreneurship* (1991).

7. Butler, *Entrepreneurship* (2005).

8. Butler, *Entrepreneurship* (2005), 119. Alonzo Herndon was one of the most successful of these early black entrepreneurs in the insurance industry.

9. The Freedman's Bank was one of the most successful and important black-owned banks that was dedicated to lending money to blacks.

10. Robert Boyd, "The Storefront Church Ministry in African American Communities of the Urban North During the Great Migration: The Making of an Ethnic Niche," *Social Science Journal* 35, no. 3 (1998): 319–33.

11. Butler, *Entrepreneurship* (2005).

12. William Harvey and Eugene Anderson, *Minorities in Higher Education* (Washington, DC: American Council on Education, 2005).

13. Daniel Fusfield and Timothy Bates, *The Political Economy of the Urban Ghetto* (Carbondale: Southern Illinois University Press, 1984).

14. Juliet Walker, *The History of Black Business in America: Capitalism, Race, Entrepreneurship* (New York: McMillan Library Reference, 1998).

15. Walker, *The History of Black Business in America*, 290.

16. Timothy Bates, *Race, Self-Employment and Upward Mobility: An Illusive Dream* (Baltimore: Johns Hopkins Press, 1997).

17. Robert Mark Silverman, "Black Business, Group Resources, and the Economic Detour: Contemporary Black Manufacturers in Chicago's Ethnic Beauty Aids Industry," *Journal of Black Studies* 30, no. 2 (1999): 232–58.

18. Combs attended Howard University but did not complete his degree.

19. Butler, *Entrepreneurship* (2005).

20. Fusfield and Bates, *The Political Economy of the Urban Ghetto*

21. Melvin Oliver and Thomas Shapiro, *Black Wealth/White Wealth: A New Perspective on Racial Inequality* (New York: Routledge, 1995).

22. Walker, *The History of Black Business in America*, 129.

23. Butler, *Entrepreneurship* (1991); and Walker, *The History of Black Business in America*.

24. Butler, *Entrepreneurship* (2005).

25. E. Frederick Morrow, *Way Down South Up North* (Philadelphia: United Church Press, 1973).

26. Kimberly Battle-Waters, *Sheila's Shop: Working-Class African American Women Talk about Life, Love, Race and Hair* (Lanham, MD: Rowman & Littlefield, 2004), 27.

27. Morrow, *Way Down South Up North*.

28. Noliwe Rooks, *Hair Raising: Beauty, Culture and African American Women* (New Brunswick, NJ: Rutgers University Press, 1996), 135.

29. Rooks, *Hair Raising*, 33.

30. Rooks, *Hair Raising*, 51.

31. See A'Lelia Bundles, *On Her Own Ground: The Life and Times of Madam C. J. Walker* (New York: Scribner, 2001); Rooks, *Hair Raising*; and Walker, *The History of Black Business in America*.

32. Beverly Lowry, *Her Dream of Dreams: The Rise and Triumph of Madam C. J. Walker* (New York: Vintage Books, 2004).

33. Robert Boyd, "Race, Labor Market Disadvantage, and Survivalist Entrepreneurship: Black Women in the Urban North During the Great Depression," *Sociological Forum* 15, no. 4 (2000): 647–70.

34. Boyd, "Race, Labor Market Disadvantage, and Survivalist Entrepreneurship," 654.

35. Silverman, "Black Business, Group Resources, and the Economic Detour."

36. Silverman, "Black Business, Group Resources, and the Economic Detour."

37. Robert Boyd, "Black Entrepreneurship in 52 Metropolitan Areas," *Sociology and Social Research* 75, no. 3 (1991): 158–63.

38. Ayana D. Byrd and Lori L. Tharps, *Hair Story: Untangling the Roots of Black Hair in America* (New York: St. Martin's Press, 2001).

39. Robert Boyd, "The Great Migration to the North and the Rise of Ethnic Niches for African American Women in Beauty Culture and Hairdressing 1910–1920," *Sociological Focus* 29, no. 1 (1996): 33–45; Bundles, *On Her Own Ground*; and Rooks, *Hair Raising*.

40. Interview with Terri Winston, publisher of the trade magazine *Salon Sense*.

41. See Dipannita Basu and Pnina Werbner, "Bootstrap Capitalism and the Culture Industries: A Critique of Invidious Comparisons in the Study of Entrepreneurship," *Ethnic and Racial Studies* 24, no. 2 (2001): 236–62; and A. Wade Smith, "Race, Gender and Entrepreneurial Orientation," *National Journal of Sociology* 6, no. 2 (1992): 141–55.

42. This research center indicates that projected estimates are that the numbers of black women entrepreneurs have grown 147 percent between 1997 and 2006. Center for Women's Business Research, *Businesses Owned by African American Women in the United States, 2006: A Fact Sheet* (Washington, DC: Center for Women's Business Research, 2006).

43. Bonnie T. Dill, "'Making Your Job Good Yourself': Domestic Service and the Construction of Personal Dignity," in *Women and the Politics of Empowerment*, ed. Ann Bookman and Sandra Morgen (Philadelphia: Temple University Press, 1988), 33–52; and Judith Rollins, *Between Women: Domestics and Their Employers* (Philadelphia: Temple University Press, 1985).

44. See Yanick St. Jean and Joe Feagin, *Double Burden: Black Women and Everyday Racism* (Amonk, NY: M.E. Sharpe, 1998).

45. Ingrid Banks, *Hair Matters: Beauty, Power and Black Women's Consciousness* (New York: New York University Press, 2000).

Chapter 3: Business Decisions in the Racial Enclave Economy

1. Yanick St. Jean and Joe Feagin, *Double Burden: Black Women and Everyday Racism* (Amonk, NY: M.E. Sharpe, 1998).

2. St. Jean and Feagin, *Double Burden*.

3. Melissa A. Milkie, "Social Comparisons, Reflected Appraisals, and Mass Media," *Social Psychology Quarterly* 62, no. 2 (1998): 190–210; and Asali Solomon, "Black Fuzzy Thing," in *Naked: Black Women Bare All about Their Skin, Hair, Hips, Lips and Other Parts*, ed. Ayana Byrd and Akiba Solomon (New York: Penguin, 2005), 33–42.

4. bell hooks, *Black Looks: Race and Representation* (Cambridge, MA: South End Press, 1992); Imani Perry, "Who(se) Am I? The Identity and Image of Women in Hip-Hop," in *Gender, Race, and Class*, second ed., ed. Gail Dines and Jean M. Humez (Thousand Oaks, CA: Sage, 2003), 136–48.

5. Avis Thomas-Lester, "At Six Flags, the Don'ts of Dos," *The Washington Post*, June 17, 2006.

6. bel! hooks, "Straightening Our Hair," in *Reading Culture: Contexts for Critical Reading and Writing*, ed. Diana George and John Trimbur (New York: Longman, 1999), 221.

7. Ingrid Banks, "Social and Personal Constructions of Hair: Cultural Practices and Belief Systems among African-American Women," *Dissertation Abstracts International* 59, no. 3 (1998); Maxine Leeds Craig, *Ain't I a Beauty Queen? Black Women,*

Beauty, and the Politics of Culture (New York: Oxford University Press, 2002); Gloria Wade-Gayles, *Rooted Against the Wind* (Boston: Beacon Press, 1996); and Rose Weitz, "Women and Their Hair: Seeking Power Through Resistance and Accommodation," *Gender & Society* 15, no. 5 (2001): 667–86.

8. Adia Harvey, "Personal Satisfaction and Economic Improvement," *Journal of Black Studies* (March 20, 2007).

9. Midge Wilson and Kathy Russell, *Divided Sisters: Bridging the Gap Between Black Women and White Women* (New York: Doubleday, 1996). In their discussion of the ways hair is racialized as well as gendered, these authors refer to Brownmiller's statement that: "White women may have bad hair days. They do not have bad hair lives." This statement underscores how the social context that encourages women to use hair as a means of achieving beauty standards is not just gendered, but also racialized in important ways.

10. Butler, *Entrepreneurship* (1991).

11. Edna Bonacich, "A Theory of Middleman Minorities," *American Sociological Review* 38, no. 5 (1973): 583–94; Sally Ann Davies-Netzley, *Gendered Capital: Entrepreneurial Women in American Society* (New York: Garland Publishing, Inc., 2000); and Ivan H. Light and Carolyn Rosenstein, *Race, Ethnicity, and Entrepreneurship in Urban America* (New York: Aldin de Gruyter, 1995).

12. Debbie Gruenstein Bocian, Keith S. Ernst, and Wei Li, "Unfair Lending: The Effect of Race and Ethnicity on the Price of Subprime Mortgages," Center for Responsible Lending (Washington, DC: Center for Responsible Lending, 2006).

13. Melvin Oliver and Thomas Shapiro, *Black Wealth/White Wealth: A New Perspective on Racial Inequality* (New York: Routledge, 1995).

14. Oliver and Shapiro, *Black Wealth/White Wealth.*

15. Recent statistics show that 48 percent of black families are maintained by a single mother, compared with 16 percent of white families. See Jason Fields, *Children's Living Arrangements and Characteristics*, Current Population Reports Ser. P20, No. 547 (Washington, DC: U.S. Government Printing Office, 2003).

16. Cornrows and dreadlocks are not specifically gendered, since they are as likely to be worn by black men as by black women. However, black men also face less social pressure to straighten their hair than do black women. Thus, when workplace policy prohibits these hairstyles, black women may be more likely to straighten their hair as a means of conforming. This process reinforces the idea that black women's natural hair precludes them from meeting gendered, racialized standards of beauty and attractiveness.

Chapter 4: A Pathway to Financial Security

1. Christine Williams, *Inside Toyland: Working, Shopping, and Social Inequality* (Berkeley: University of California Press, 2006).

2. Irene Browne, "Latinas and African American Women in the Labor Market," in *Latinas and African American Women at Work: Race, Gender, and Economic Inequality*, ed. Irene Browne (New York: Russell Sage Foundation, 1999).

3. Ivan H. Light and Steven J. Gold, *Ethnic Economies* (San Diego: Academic Press, 2000).

4. Michael Eric Dyson, *Is Bill Cosby Right? Or Has the Black Middle Class Lost Its Mind?* (New York: Perseus, 2005).

5. For a detailed refutation of Cosby's claims, see Dyson, *Is Bill Cosby Right?*

6. Ivy Kennelly, "'That Single Mother Element': How White Employers Typify Black Women," *Gender & Society* 13, no. 2 (1999): 168–92; Joleen Kirschenmen and Kathryn M. Neckerman, "'We'd Love to Hire Them But . . .' The Meaning of Race for Employers," in *Rethinking the Color Line: Readings in Race and Ethicity*, ed. Charles A. Gallagher. (New York: McGraw-Hill, 2006), 306–17; Jonathan Kozol, *Savage Inequalities: Children in America's Schools* (New York: Crown Publishing, 1991); and William J. Wilson, *The Truly Disadvantaged: The Inner City, The Underclass, and Public Policy* (Chicago: University of Chicago Press, 1987).

7. Mary Corcoran, "The Economic Progress of African American Women," in *Latinas and African American Women at Work: Race, Gender, and Economic Inequality* ed. Irene Browne (New York: Russell Sage Foundation, 1999), 35–60.

8. Alice Kemp, *Women's Work: Degraded and Devalued* (Englewood Cliffs, NJ: Prentice Hall, 1993).

9. Kennelly, "That Single Mother Element."

10. Patricia Hill Collins, *Black Sexual Politics: African Americans, Gender, and the New Racism* (New York: Routledge, 2004), 137. See also Tim Brezina, "What Went Wrong in New Orleans? An Examination of the Welfare Dependency Explanation," unpublished manuscript, Department of Criminal Justice, Georgia State University, 2006.

11. Black women earn 67 percent of bachelor, 69 percent of master's degrees, 66 percent of doctoral degrees, and 58 percent of professional degrees awarded to African Americans. See Sharlene Hesse-Biber and Gregg Lee Carter, *Working Women in America: Split Dreams* (New York: Oxford University Press, 2000); and Michael J. Smith and Michael K. Fleming, "African American Parents in the Search Stage of College Choice: Unintentional Contributions to the Female to Male College Enrollment Gap," *Urban Education* 41, no. 1 (2006): 71–102.

12. Hesse-Biber and Carter, *Working Women in America*; and Kevin Stainback, "Politics, Environmental Uncertainty and Organizational Change: Race and Sex Workplace Opportunity in the Post–Civil Rights Era, 1966–2002," *Dissertation Abstracts International* 66, no. 10 (2006).

13. Statistics: Physicians: white male 37.4 percent, black male 1.3 percent, White female 10.1 percent, Black female 1.1 percent. RNS: white 86.6 percent, black 4.9 percent (Darby Steiger, Sara Bausch, Bryan Johnson, and Anne Petersen, "The Registered Nurse Population: Findings from the 2004 National Sample Survey of Registered Nurses," U.S. Department of Health and Human Services, Health Resources and Services Administration, Bureau of Health Professions, Washington, DC, 2006). LPNs (second grade of nursing): black females 17.9 percent. Nurses aides, orderlies

attendants: black females 27.0 percent. See Evelyn Nakano Glenn, "From Servitude to Service Work: Historical Continuities In the Racial Division of Paid Reproductive Labor," *Signs: Journal of Women in Culture and Society* 18, no. 1 (1992): 1–43.

14. Timothy Bates, *Race, Self-Employment and Upward Mobility: An Illusive Dream* (Baltimore: Johns Hopkins Press, 1997).

15. Scott Sernau, *Worlds Apart: Social Inequality in a New Century* (Thousand Oaks, CA: Pine Forge Press, 2001).

16. Michelle J. Budig, "Gender, Self-Employment, and Earnings: The Interlocking Structures of Family and Professional Status," *Gender & Society* 20, no. 6 (2006): 725–53.

Chapter 5: Stereotypes and Social Support

1. Joe Feagin, *Systemic Racism: A Theory of Oppression* (New York: Routledge, 2006).

2. Yanick St. Jean and Joe Feagin, *Double Burden: Black Women and Everyday Racism* (Amonk, NY: M.E. Sharpe, 1998).

3. Ella Bell and Stella Nkomo, *Our Separate Ways* (Boston: Harvard Business School Press, 2001); and Audrey Edwards, "The New Office Politics," *Essence* magazine, March 2005.

4. Elizabeth Higginbotham, *Too Much to Ask: Black Women in the Era of Integration* (Chapel Hill, NC: University of North Carolina Press, 2001).

5. William J. Wilson, *The Truly Disadvantaged: The Inner City, the Underclass, and Public Policy* (Chicago: University of Chicago Press, 1987).

6. Adolphus G. Belk, "A New Generation of Native Sons: Men of Color and the Prison Industrial Complex," paper published by Joint Center for Political and Economic Studies (Washington, DC, 2006); Michael Eric Dyson, *Is Bill Cosby Right? Or Has the Black Middle Class Lost Its Mind?* (New York: Perseus, 2005).

7. Erica Chito Childs, "Looking Behind Stereotypes of the 'Angry Black Woman.'" *Gender & Society* 19, no. 4 (2005): 544–61.

8. Katrina Bell McDonald, "Black Activist Mothering," *Gender and Society* 11, no. 6 (1997): 773–95; and Deborah Gray White, *Ar'n't I a Woman? Female Slaves in the Plantation South* (New York: W.W. Norton, 1999).

9. Dyson, *Is Bill Cosby Right?*; White, *Ar'n't I a Woman?*

10. Adia M. Harvey, "Becoming Entrepreneurs," *Gender & Society* 19, no. 6 (2005): 789–812.

11. bell hooks, *Black Looks: Race and Representation* (Cambridge, MA: South End Press, 1992), 42.

12. Higginbotham, *Too Much to Ask*; Mary Alfred, "Success in the Ivory Tower," in *Sisters of the Academy*, ed. Reitumetse Obakeng Mabokela and Anna L. Green (Sterling, VA: Stylus Press, 2001), 57–80.

13. hooks, *Black Looks*, 42.

14. W. J. Musa Moore-Foster, "Up from Brutality: Freeing Black Communities from Sexual Violence," in *Transforming a Rape Culture*, ed. Emilie Buchwald, Pamela Fletcher, and Martha Roth (Minneapolis: Milkweed Press, 1993), 417–26.

15. St. Jean and Feagin, *Double Burden*.

16. Bonnie T. Dill, "'Making Your Job Good Yourself': Domestic Service and the Construction of Personal Dignity," in *Women and the Politics of Empowerment*, ed. Ann Bookman and Sandra Morgen (Philadelphia: Temple University Press, 1988), 33–52; and Judith Rollins, *Between Women: Domestics and Their Employers* (Philadelphia: Temple University Press, 1985).

17. Dill, "Making Your Job Good Yourself."

18. Bell and Nkomo, *Our Separate Ways*; and Joe Feagin and Melvin Sikes, *Living with Racism: The Black Middle Class Experience* (Boston: Beacon Press, 1994).

19. Feagin and Sikes (1994) offer one particularly interesting example of black women being forced to display exceptional capabilities in order for white colleagues to consider them barely competent. They cite a story of a sales executive who outperforms everyone in her unit only to be given an evaluation of "G" (which indicates that her performance is good). When this employee refuses to accept this evaluation and explains her exemplary record, her supervisor reconsiders and upgrades her evaluation to an "O" (which signifies that her performance is outstanding).

20. Eduardo Bonilla-Silva, *White Supremacy and Racism in the Post–Civil Rights Era* (Boulder, CO: Lynne Rienner Publishers, 2001); and Michael Omi and Howard Winant, *Racial Formation in the United States from the 1960s to the 1980s* (New York: Routledge, 1986).

21. Feagin, *Systemic Racism*.

22. Bonilla-Silva, *White Supremacy and Racism*; and Feagin, *Systemic Racism*.

23. Roxana Harlow, "'Race doesn't matter, but . . .': The Effect of Race on Professors' Experiences and Emotion Management in the Undergraduate College Classroom," *Social Psychology Quarterly* 66, no. 4 (2003): 348–63; and St. Jean and Feagin, *Double Burden*.

24. Eduardo Bonilla-Silva, *Racism Without Racists: Color Blind Racism and the Persistence of Racial Inequality in the United States* (Lanham, MD: Rowman & Littlefield, 2003); and Feagin, *Systemic Racism*.

25. Bonilla-Silva, *Racism Without Racists*; Feagin, *Systemic Racism*; Joe Feagin and Hernan Vera, *White Racism: The Basics* (New York: Routledge, 1995); Ann Arnett Ferguson, *Bad Boys: Public Schools in the Making of Black Masculinity* (Ann Arbor: University of Michigan Press, 2000); and Donald Tomaskovic-Devey, *Gender and Racial Inequality at Work: The Sources and Consequences of Job Segregation* (Ithaca, NY: ILR Press, 1993).

Chapter 6: Ethnic Divisions in the Racial Enclave

1. Some braiding salons include employees who will twist a customer's hair into dreadlocks. While I did not interview any owners who offered this service, it is available in some braiding and natural-hair salons.

2. Eunju Lee, *Gendered Processes: Korean Immigrant Small Business Ownership* (New York: LFB Scholarly Publishing, 2006); and Alejandro Portes and Leif Jensen, "The Enclave and the Entrants: Patterns of Ethnic Enterprise in Miami Before and After Mariel," *American Sociological Review* 54, no. 6 (1989): 929–49.

3. M. Patricia Fernandez-Kelly and Anna M. Garcia, "Power Surrendered, Power Restored: The Politics of Home and Work among Hispanic Women in Southern California and Southern Florida," in *Women, Politics and Change*, ed. Louise Tilly and Patricia Guerin (New York: Russell Sage Foundation, 1990), 130–49; Portes and Jensen, "The Enclave and the Entrants."

4. Ivan H. Light and Carolyn Rosenstein, *Race, Ethnicity, and Entrepreneurship in Urban America* (New York: Aldin de Gruyter, 1995).

5. Portes and Jensen, "The Enclave and the Entrants."

6. Edna Bonacich, "A Theory of Middleman Minorities," *American Sociological Review* 38, no. 5 (1973): 583–94; and Light and Rosenstein, *Race, Ethnicity, and Entrepreneurship*.

7. Lee (2006) has argued that these tensions are overstated.

8. Mary Waters, *Black Identities: West Indian Immigrant Dreams and American Realities* (Cambridge, MA: Harvard University Press, 2001).

9. Drucilla Barker and Susan Feiner, *Liberating Economics: Feminist Perspectives on Family, Work, and Globalization* (Ann Arbor: University of Michigan Press, 2004).

10. T. Scarlett Epstein, "Female Petty Entrepreneurs and Their Multiple Roles," in *Women in Business*, ed. Sheila Allen and Carole Truman (London: Routledge, 1993), 14–27; Sherri Grasmuck and Rosario Espinal, "Market Success or Female Autonomy? Income, Ideology, and Empowerment among Microentrepreneurs in the Dominican Republic," *Gender & Society* 14, no. 2 (2000): 231–55; and Sidney Mintz, "The Employment of Capital by Market Women in Haiti," in *Capital, Saving and Credit in Peasant Societies*, ed. Raymond Firth and B. S. Yamey (Chicago: Aldine Publishing, 1962), 256–86.

11. This is true for women of color in peripheral and semiperipheral countries also.

12. Gloria Wade-Gayles, *Rooted Against the Wind* (Boston: Beacon Press, 1996).

13. In black American communities, many young girls wear their hair braided. Getting old enough to have their hair straightened is often considered a rite of passage. Ingrid Banks, *Hair Matters: Beauty, Power and Black Women's Consciousness* (New York: New York University Press, 2000); and bell hooks, *Feminist Theory: From Margin to Center*, second ed. (Cambridge, MA: South End Press, 2000).

14. Ella Bell and Stella Nkomo, *Our Separate Ways* (Boston: Harvard Business School Press, 2001); Cherisse Jones and Kumea Shorter-Gooden, *Shifting: The Double Lives of Black Women in America* (New York: Harper Perennial, 2000); and Yanick St. Jean and Joe Feagin, *Double Burden: Black Women and Everyday Racism* (Amonk, NY: M.E. Sharpe, 1998).

15. For more discussion of this stereotype, please refer to Patricia Hill Collins, *Black Sexual Politics* (New York: Routledge, 2004).

16. Lee, *Gendered Processes*; Waters, *Ethnic Options*.

17. Bonacich, "A Theory of Middleman Minorities."

Chapter 7: Conclusion

1. Philomena Essed, *Understanding Everyday Racism* (Newbury Park, CA: Sage, 1991).

2. Patricia Hill Collins, *Black Feminist Thought* (New York: Routledge, 2000); *Black Sexual Politics: African Americans, Gender, and the New Racism* (New York: Routledge, 2004); and Yen Le Espiritu, *Asian American Women and Men: Labor, Laws and Love* (Thousand Oaks, CA: Sage, 1997).

3. Eduardo Bonilla-Silva, *Racism Without Racists: Color Blind Racism and the Persistence of Racial Inequality in the United States* (Lanham, MD: Rowman & Littlefield, 2003).

4. Feagin, *Systemic Racism: A Theory of Oppression* (New York: Routledge, 2006).

5. Timothy Bates, *Race, Self-Employment and Upward Mobility: An Illusive Dream* (Baltimore: Johns Hopkins Press, 1997).

6. John S. Butler, *Entrepreneurship and Self-Help among Black Americans: A Reconsideration of Race and Economics*, second edition (New York: SUNY Press, 2005); and Bart Landry, *The New Black Middle Class* (Berkeley: University of California Press, 1987).

7. Alejandro Portes and Robert Bach, *Latin Journey: Cuban and Mexican Immigrants in the United States* (Berkeley: University of California Press, 1985); and Jimy M. Sanders and Victor Nee, "Limits of Ethnic Solidarity in the Enclave Economy," *American Sociological Review* 52, no. 6 (1987): 745–67.

8. Sally Ann Davies-Netzley, *Gendered Capital: Entrepreneurial Women in American Society* (New York: Garland Publishing, Inc., 2000).

9. Bates, *Race, Self-Employment and Upward Mobility*.

10. Minority Business Development Agency, "Mission Statement," posted March 31, 2005, accessed May 15, 2007. http://www.mbda.gov/?section_id=2&bucket_id=643&content_id=3145&well=entire_page.

11. Minority Business Development Agency, "Mission Statement."

12. "Major Accomplishments of the U.S. Senate, 108th Congress, second session, to date," posted July 22, 2004, accessed May 15, 2007, author Jon Kyl. http://rpc.senate.gov/_files/108Accomplishments072204.pdf.

13. The Whitaker Group, "Rosa Whitaker Brings U.S. Apparel Industry Giant Martin Trust to Ghana and Uganda," posted July 27, 2004, accessed May 15, 2007. http://allafrica.com/stories/200407270001.html8.

14. Drucilla Barker and Susan Feiner, *Liberating Economics: Feminist Perspectives on Family, Work, and Globalization* (Ann Arbor: University of Michigan Press, 2004); and Jody Heymann, *Forgotten Families: Ending the Growing Crisis Confronting Children and Working Parents in the Global Economy* (New York: Oxford University Press, 2006).

15. Michael K. Brown, Martin Carnoy, Elliott Currie, Troy Duster, David B. Oppenheimer, Marjorie B. Schultz, and David Wellman, *Whitewashing Race: The Myth of a Color-Blind Society* (Berkeley: University of California Press, 2003), 248.

16. Maria Charles and David Grusky, *Occupational Ghettos: The Worldwide Segregation of Women and Men* (Palo Alto, CA: Stanford University Press, 2005); and Barbara Reskin and Patricia Roos, *Job Queues, Gender Queues* (Philadelphia: Temple University Press, 1990).

17. Joya Misra, "Latinas and African American Women in the Labor Market: Implications for Policy," in *Latinas and African American Women at Work: Race, Gender, and Economic Inequality*, ed. Irene Browne (New York: Russell Sage Foundation, 1999), 408–32.

18. Bonilla-Silva, *White Supremacy and Racism in the Post-Civil Rights Era* (Boulder, CO: Lynn Rienner Publishers, 2001); and Feagin, *Systemic Racism*.

Appendix: Methodology

1. Michael Burawoy, Alice Burson, Ann Ferguson, and Kathryn J. Fox, *Ethnology Unbound: Power and Resistance in the Modern Metropolis* (Berkeley: University of California Press, 1991), 279.

2. For two important exceptions, see Sally Ann Davies-Netzley, *Gendered Capital: Entrepreneurial Women in American Society* (New York: Garland Publishing, Inc., 2000), and Eunju Lee, *Gendered Processes: Korean Immigrant Small Business Ownership* (New York: LFB Scholarly Publishing, 2006).

3. Kimberly Battle-Waters, *Sheila's Shop: Working-Class African American Women Talk about Life, Love, Race and Hair* (Lanham, MD: Rowman & Littlefield, 2004).

4. Battle-Waters, *Sheila's Shop*, 109.

References

Aldrich, Howard, and Roger Waldinger. 1990. "Ethnicity and Entrepreneurs." *American Review of Sociology* 16: 111–35.

Alfred, Mary. 2001. "Success in the Ivory Tower," in *Sisters of the Academy*, ed. Reitumetse Obakeng Mabokela and Anna L. Green. Sterling, VA: Stylus Press, 57–80.

Banks, Ingrid. 1998. Social and Personal Constructions of Hair: Cultural Practices and Belief Systems among African-American Women. *Dissertation Abstracts International* 59, no. 3, 966A (UMI No. 9828593).

———. 2000. *Hair Matters: Beauty, Power and Black Women's Consciousness*. New York: New York University Press.

Barker, Drucilla, and Susan Feiner. 2004. *Liberating Economics: Feminist Perspectives on Family, Work, and Globalization*. Ann Arbor: University of Michigan Press.

Basu, Dipannita, and Pnina Werbner. 2001. "Bootstrap Capitalism and the Culture Industries: A Critique of Invidious Comparisons in the Study of Entrepreneurship." *Ethnic and Racial Studies* 24, no. 2: 236–62.

Bates, Timothy. 1997. *Race, Self-Employment and Upward Mobility: An Illusive Dream*. Baltimore: Johns Hopkins Press.

Battle-Waters, Kimberly. 2004. *Sheila's Shop: Working-Class African American Women Talk about Life, Love, Race and Hair*. Lanham, MD: Rowman & Littlefield.

Belk, Adolphus G. 2006. A New Generation of Native Sons: Men of Color and the Prison Industrial Complex. Paper published by Joint Center for Political and Economic Studies.

Bell, Ella, and Stella Nkomo. 2001. *Our Separate Ways*. Boston: Harvard Business School Press.

Blalock, Hubert M. 1967. *Toward a Theory of Minority-group Relations*. New York: Wiley.

Bocian, Debbie Gruenstein, Keith Ernst, and Wei Li. 2006. "Unfair Lending: The Effect of Race and Ethnicity on the Price of Subprime Mortgages." Washington, DC: Center for Responsible Lending. Available at http://www.responsiblelending.org/press/statements/page.jsp?itemID=29194107.

Bonacich, Edna. 1973. "A Theory of Middleman Minorities." *American Sociological Review* 38, no. 5: 583–94.

Bonacich, Edna, and John Modell. 1980. *The Economic Basis of Solidarity: Small Business in the Japanese American Community*. Berkeley: University of California Press.

Bonilla-Silva, Eduardo. 2001. *White Supremacy and Racism in the Post–Civil Rights Era*. Boulder, CO: Lynne Rienner Publishers.

———. 2003. *Racism Without Racists: Color Blind Racism and the Persistence of Racial Inequality in the United States*. Lanham, MD: Rowman & Littlefield.

Boyd, Robert. 1991. "Black Entrepreneurship in 52 Metropolitan Areas." *Sociology and Social Research* 75, no. 3: 158–63.

———. 1996. "The Great Migration to the North and the Rise of Ethnic Niches for African American Women in Beauty Culture and Hairdressing 1910–1920." *Sociological Focus* 29, no. 1: 33–45.

———. 1998. "The Storefront Church Ministry in African American Communities of the Urban North During the Great Migration: The Making of an Ethnic Niche." *Social Science Journal* 35, no. 3: 319–33.

———. 2000. "Race, Labor Market Disadvantage, and Survivalist Entrepreneurship: Black Women in the Urban North During the Great Depression." *Sociological Forum* 15, no. 4: 647–70.

Brezina, Tim. 2006. What Went Wrong in New Orleans? An Examination of the Welfare Dependency Explanation. Unpublished manuscript, Department of Criminal Justice, Georgia State University.

Brown, Michael K., Martin Carnoy, Elliott Currie, Troy Duster, David B. Oppenheimer, Marjorie B. Schultz, and David Wellman. 2003. *Whitewashing Race: The Myth of a Color-Blind Society*. Berkeley: University of California Press.

Browne, Irene. 1999. "Latinas and African American Women in the Labor Market." In *Latinas and African American Women at Work: Race, Gender, and Economic Inequality*, ed. Irene Browne. New York: Russell Sage Foundation, 1–33.

Budig, Michelle J. 2006. "Gender, Self-Employment, and Earnings: The Interlocking Structures of Family and Professional Status." *Gender & Society* 20, no. 6: 725–53.

Bundles, A'Lelia. 2001. *On Her Own Ground: The Life and Times of Madam C. J. Walker*. New York: Scribner.

Burawoy, Michael, Alice Burson, Ann Ferguson, and Kathryn J. Fox. 1991. *Ethnology Unbound: Power and Resistance in the Modern Metropolis*. Berkeley: University of California Press.

Bush, George W. 2004. *The Challenge: America's Changing Society*. Speech to the National Federation of Independent Businesses. June 17. Washington, DC.

Butler, John S. 1991. *Entrepreneurship and Self-Help among Black Americans: A Reconsideration of Race and Economics*. Albany, NY: SUNY Press.

———. 2005. *Entrepreneurship and Self-Help among Black Americans: A Reconsideration of Race and Economics*, 2nd ed. Albany, NY: SUNY Press.

Byrd, Ayana D. and Lori L. Tharps. 2001. *Hair Story: Untangling the Roots of Black Hair in America*. New York: St. Martin's Press.

Center for Women's Business Research. 2004. *African American Women-Owned Businesses in the United States, 2004: A Fact Sheet*. Washington, DC: Center for Women's Business Research.

———. 2006. *Businesses Owned by African American Women in the United States, 2006: A Fact Sheet*. Washington, DC: Center for Women's Business Research.

Chan, Sucheng. 1994. *Hmong Means Free: Life in Laos and America*. Philadelphia: Temple University Press.

Charles, Maria, and David Grusky. 2005. *Occupational Ghettos: The Worldwide Segregation of Women and Men*. Palo Alto, CA: Stanford University Press.

Childs, Erica Chito. 2005. Looking Behind Stereotypes of the "Angry Black Woman." *Gender & Society* 19, no. 4: 544–61.

Cole, Johnetta B., and Beverly Guy-Sheftall. 2003. *Gender Talk: The Struggle for Women's Equality in African American Communities*. New York: One World/Ballantine.

Collins, Patricia Hill. 1990. *Black Feminist Thought*. New York: Routledge.

———. 2000. *Black Feminist Thought*, second ed. New York: Routledge.

———. 2004. *Black Sexual Politics: African Americans, Gender, and the New Racism*. New York: Routledge.

Corcoran, Mary. 1999. "The Economic Progress of African American Women." In *Latinas and African American Women at Work: Race, Gender, and Economic Inequality*, ed. Irene Browne. New York: Russell Sage Foundation, 35–60.

Cose, Ellis. 1993. *The Rage of a Privileged Class*. New York: HarperCollins.

Craig, Maxine Leeds. 2002. *Ain't I a Beauty Queen? Black Women, Beauty, and the Politics of Culture*. New York: Oxford University Press.

Davies-Netzley, Sally Ann. 2000. *Gendered Capital: Entrepreneurial Women in American Society*. New York: Garland Publishing, Inc.

Davis, Angela. 1981. *Women, Race, and Class*. New York: Random House.

Dill, Bonnie T. 1988. " 'Making Your Job Good Yourself': Domestic Service and the Construction of Personal Dignity." In *Women and the Politics of Empowerment*, ed. Ann Bookman and Sandra Morgen. Philadelphia: Temple University Press, 33–52.

———. 1993. *Across the Boundaries of Race and Class: An Exploration of Work and Family Among Black Female Domestic Servants*. New York: Routledge.

Durr, Marlene, and John R. Logan. 1997. "Racial Submarkets in Government Employment: African American Managers in New York State." *Sociological Forum* 12, no. 3: 353–70.

Dyson, Michael Eric. 2005. *Is Bill Cosby Right? Or Has the Black Middle Class Lost Its Mind?* New York: Perseus.

Edwards, Audrey. 2005. "The New Office Politics." *Essence* magazine, March.

Epstein, T. Scarlett. 1993. "Female Petty Entrepreneurs and their Multiple Roles." In *Women in Business*, edited by Sheila Allen and Carole Truman. London: Routledge, 14–27.

Espiritu, Yen Le. 1997. *Asian American Women and Men: Labor, Laws and Love.* Thousand Oaks, CA: Sage.

Essed, Philomena. 1991. *Understanding Everyday Racism.* Newbury Park, CA: Sage.

Feagin, Joe. 2000. *Racist America.* New York: Routledge.

———. 2006. *Systemic Racism: A Theory of Oppression.* New York: Routledge.

Feagin, Joe, and Eileen O'Brien. 2003. *White Men on Race: Power, Privilege, and the Shaping of Cultural Consciousness.* Boston: Beacon Press.

Feagin, Joe, and Melvin Sikes. 1994. *Living with Racism: The Black Middle Class Experience.* Boston: Beacon Press.

Feagin, Joe, and Hernan Vera. 1995. *White Racism: The Basics.* New York: Routledge.

Feagin, Joe, Hernan Vera, and Nikitah Imani. 1996. *The Agony of Education: Black Students at White Colleges and Universities.* New York: Routledge.

Ferguson, Ann Arnett. 2000. *Bad Boys: Public Schools in the Making of Black Masculinity.* Ann Arbor: University of Michigan Press.

Fernandez-Kelly, M. Patricia, and Anna M. Garcia. 1990. "Power Surrendered, Power Restored: The Politics of Home and Work Among Hispanic Women in Southern California and Southern Florida." In *Women, Politics and Change*, ed. Louise Tilly and Patricia Guerin. New York: Russell Sage Foundation, 130–49.

Fields, Jason. 2003. *Children's Living Arrangements and Characteristics.* Current Population Reports Ser. P20, No. 547. Washington, DC: U.S. Government Printing Office. http://pur/.access.gpo/GPO/LPS33039.

Foner, Eric. 2002. *Who Owns History?* New York: Hill and Wang.

Frazier, E. Franklin. 1957. *Black Bourgeoisie: The Rise of a New Middle Class in the United States.* Glencoe, IL: The Free Press.

Fusfield, Daniel, and Timothy Bates. 1984. *The Political Economy of the Urban Ghetto.* Carbondale: Southern Illinois University Press.

Glenn, Evelyn Nakano. 1992. "From Servitude to Service Work: Historical Continuities in the Racial Division of Paid Reproductive Labor." *Signs: Journal of Women in Culture and Society* 18, no. 1: 1–43.

Grasmuck, Sherri, and Rosario Espinal. 2000. Market Success or Female Autonomy? Income, Ideology, and Empowerment among Microentrepreneurs in the Dominican Republic. *Gender & Society* 14, no. 2: 231–55.

Harlow, Roxana. 2003. "'Race doesn't matter, but . . . ': The effect of race on professors' experiences and emotion management in the undergraduate college classroom." *Social Psychology Quarterly* 66, no. 4: 348–63.

Harris, Albert. 1936. "Political, Racial and Differential Psychology." *Journal of Social Psychology* 7: 474–79.

Harvey, Adia M. 2005. "Becoming Entrepreneurs." *Gender & Society* 19, no. 6: 789–812.

———. 2007. Personal Satisfaction and Economic Improvement. *Journal of Black Studies*. March 20, 2007. DOI: 10.1177/0123456789123456.

Harvey, William, and Eugene Anderson. 2005. Minorities in Higher Education. Washington, DC: American Council on Education.

Hesse-Biber, Sharlene, and Gregg Lee Carter. 2000. *Working Women in America: Split Dreams*. New York: Oxford University Press.

Heymann, Jody. 2006. *Forgotten Families: Ending the Growing Crisis Confronting Children and Working Parents in the Global Economy*. New York: Oxford University Press.

Higginbotham, Elizabeth. 2001. *Too Much to Ask: Black Women in the Era of Integration*. Chapel Hill: University of North Carolina Press.

hooks, bell. 1992. *Black Looks: Race and Representation*. Cambridge, MA: South End Press.

———. 1999. "Straightening Our Hair." In Diana George and John Trimbur (ed.) *Reading Culture: Contexts for Critical Reading and Writing*. New York: Longman, 220–25.

———. 2000. *Feminist Theory: From Margin to Center*. Second edition. Cambridge, MA: South End Press.

Hopkins, Jim. 2006. "African American Women Step up in Business World." *USA Today*, Aug. 24.

Hutchinson, Earl Ofari. 1970. *The Myth of Black Capitalism*. New York: Monthly Review Press.

Jones, Cherisse, and Kumea Shorter-Gooden. 2000. *Shifting: The Double Lives of Black Women in America*. New York: Harper Perennial.

Kemp, Alice. 1993. *Women's Work: Degraded and Devalued*. Englewood Cliffs, NJ: Prentice Hall.

Kennelly, Ivy. 1999. "'That Single Mother Element': How White Employers Typify Black Women." *Gender & Society* 13, no. 2: 168–92.

King, Deborah K. "Multiple Jeopardy, Multiple Consciousness: The Context of a Black Feminist Ideology." *Signs: Journal of Women in Culture and Society* 14, no. 1 (1988): 42–72.

Kirschenmen, Joleen, and Kathryn M. Neckerman. 2006. "'We'd Love to Hire Them But . . .': The Meaning of Race for Employers." In *Rethinking the Color Line: Readings in Race and Ethnicity*, ed. Charles A. Gallagher. New York: McGraw Hill, 306–17.

Kozol, Jonathan. 1991. *Savage Inequalities: Children in America's Schools*. New York: Crown Publishing.

Landry, Bart. 1987. *The New Black Middle Class*. Berkeley: University of California Press.

Lee, Eunju. 2006. *Gendered Processes: Korean Immigrant Small Business Ownership*. New York: LFB Scholarly Publishing.

Lee, Jennifer. 2002. From Civil Relations to Racial Conflict: Merchant-Customer Interactions in Urban America. *American Sociological Review* 67, no. 1: 77–98.

Lee, Stacey. 1996. *Unraveling the Model Minority Stereotype*. New York: Teachers College Press.

Lersch, Kim, and Joe Feagin. 1996. "Violent Police-Citizen Encounters: An Analysis of Major Newspaper Accounts." *Critical Sociology* 22: 29–49.

Light, Ivan H. 1972. *Ethnic Enterprise in America*. Berkeley: University of California Press.

Light, Ivan H., and Steven J. Gold. 2000. *Ethnic Economies*. San Diego: Academic Press.

Light, Ivan H., and Carolyn Rosenstein. 1995. *Race, Ethnicity, and Entrepreneurship in Urban America*. New York: Aldin de Gruyter.

Lorber, Judith. 2001. "Night to His Day: The Social Construction of Gender." In *Men and Masculinity*, ed. Theodore F. Cohen. Belmont, CA: Wadsworth, 19–28.

Lowry, Beverly. 2004. *Her Dream of Dreams: The Rise and Triumph of Madam C. J. Walker*. New York: Vintage Books.

McDonald, Katrina Bell. 1997. "Black Activist Mothering." *Gender and Society* 11, no. 6: 773–95.

Milkie, Melissa A. 1998. "Social Comparisons, Reflected Appraisals, and Mass Media." *Social Psychology Quarterly* 62, no. 2: 190–210.

Min, Pyong Gap. 1996. *Caught in the Middle: Korean Merchants in America's Multi-Ethnic Cities*. Berkeley: University of California Press.

Minority Business Development Agency Mission Statement, posted March 31, 2005, accessed May 15, 2007. http://www.mbda.gov/?section_id=2&bucket_id=643&content_id=3145&well=entire_page.

Mintz, Sidney. 1962. "The Employment of Capital by Market Women in Haiti." In *Capital, Saving and Credit in Peasant Societies*, ed. Raymond Firth and B. S. Yamey. Chicago: Aldine Publishing, 256–86.

Misra, Joya. 1999. "Latinas and African American Women in the Labor Market: Implications for Policy." In *Latinas and African American Women at Work: Race, Gender, and Economic Inequality*, ed. Irene Browne. New York: Russell Sage Foundation, 408–32.

Moore-Foster, W. J. Musa. 1993. "Up from Brutality: Freeing Black Communities from Sexual Violence." In *Transforming a Rape Culture*, ed. Emilie Buchwald, Pamela Fletcher, and Martha Roth. Minneapolis, MN: Milkweed Press, 417–26.

Morrow, E. Frederick. 1973. *Way Down South Up North*. Philadelphia: United Church Press.

Oliver, Melvin, and Thomas Shapiro. 1995. *Black Wealth/White Wealth: A New Perspective on Racial Inequality*: New York: Routledge.

Omi, Michael, and Howard Winant. 1986. *Racial Formation in the United States from the 1960s to the 1980s*. New York: Routledge.

Perry, Imani. 2003. "Who(se) Am I? The Identity and Image of Women in Hip-Hop." In *Gender, Race, and Class*, second edition, ed. Gail Dines and Jean M. Humez. Thousand Oaks, CA: Sage, 136–48.

Pierce, Jennifer L. 1995. *Gender Trials: Emotional Lives in Contemporary Law Firms.* Berkeley: University of California Press.

Portes, Alejandro, and Robert Bach. 1985. *Latin Journey: Cuban and Mexican Immigrants in the United States.* Berkeley: University of California Press.

Portes, Alejandro, and Leif Jensen. 1989. "The Enclave and the Entrants: Patterns of Ethnic Enterprise in Miami Before and After Mariel." *American Sociological Review* 54, no. 6: 929–49.

Portes, Alejandro, and Min Zhou. 1996. "Self-Employment and the Earnings of Immigrants." *American Sociological Review* 61, no. 2: 219–30.

Reskin, Barbara, and Patricia Roos. 1990. *Job Queues, Gender Queues.* Philadelphia: Temple University Press.

Rollins, Judith. 1985. *Between Women: Domestics and Their Employers.* Philadelphia: Temple University Press.

Rooks, Noliwe. 1996. *Hair Raising: Beauty, Culture and African American Women.* New Brunswick, NJ: Rutgers University Press.

Sanders, Jimy M., and Victor Nee. 1987. "Limits of Ethnic Solidarity in the Enclave Economy." *American Sociological Review* 52, no. 6: 745–67.

Sernau, Scott. 2001. *Worlds Apart: Social Inequality in a New Century.* Thousand Oaks, CA: Pine Forge Press.

Shapiro, Tom. 2004. *The Hidden Costs of Being African-American.* London: Oxford.

Silverman, Robert Mark. 1999. "Black Business, Group Resources, and the Economic Detour: Contemporary Black Manufacturers in Chicago's Ethnic Beauty Aids Industry." *Journal of Black Studies* 30, no. 2: 232–58.

Simmonds, Yussef. 2006. Interview with Andrew Young. *The Los Angeles Sentinel,* August 12.

Smith, A. Wade. 1992. "Race, Gender and Entrepreneurial Orientation." *National Journal of Sociology* 6, no. 2: 141–55.

Smith, Michael J., and Michael K. Fleming. 2006. "African American Parents in the Search Stage of College Choice: Unintentional Contributions to the Female to Male College Enrollment Gap." *Urban Education* 41, no. 1: 71–102.

Solomon, Asali. 2005. "Black Fuzzy Thing." In *Naked: Black Women Bare All About Their Skin, Hair, Hips, Lips and Other Parts.* Ed. Ayana Byrd and Akiba Solomon. New York: Penguin Group, 33–42.

St. Jean, Yanick, and Joe Feagin. 1998. *Double Burden: Black Women and Everyday Racism.* Amonk, NY: M.E. Sharpe.

Stainback, Kevin. 2006. Politics, Environmental Uncertainty and Organizational Change: Race and Sex Workplace Opportunity in the Post–Civil Rights Era 1966–2002. *Dissertation Abstracts International* 66, no. 10, 3826A. (UMI No. 200621989).

Steiger, Darby, Sara Bausch, Bryan Johnson, and Anne Petersen. 2004. "The Registered Nurse Population: Findings from the 2004 National Sample Survey of Registered Nurses." Published by the U.S. Department of Health and Human Services, Health Resources and Services Administration, Bureau of Health Professions. Washington, DC.

Taylor, T. Shawn. 2005. "Wall Street and Business Wednesdays: Self-Styled Entrepreneurs: Salon Ownership Affords African American Women a Comfortable Living," BlackElectorate.com, posted April 13, 2005, accessed May 15, 2007. http://www.blackelectorate.com/articles.asp?ID=1348.

Thierry, Mary. 2002. "Who Protects and Serves Me?" *Gender and Society* 16(4): 524–45.

Thomas-Lester, Avis. 2006. "At Six Flags, the Don'ts of Dos." [Electronic Version]. *The Washington Post*, June 17.

Tomaskovic-Devey, Donald. 1993. *Gender and Racial Inequality at Work: The Sources and Consequences of Job Segregation*. Ithaca, NY: ILR Press.

U.S. Senate. Major Accomplishments of the U.S. Senate, 108th Congress, second session, to date, posted July 22, 2004, accessed May 15, 2007, author Jon Kyl. http://rpc.senate.gov/_files/108Accomplishments072204.pdf.

Wade-Gayles, Gloria. 1996. *Rooted Against the Wind*. Boston: Beacon Press.

Walker, Juliet. 1998. *The History of Black Business in America: Capitalism, Race, Entrepreneurship*. New York: McMillan Library Reference.

Waters, Mary. 2001. *Black Identities: West Indian Immigrant Dreams and American Realities*. Cambridge, MA: Harvard University Press.

Weitz, Rose. 2001. "Women and Their Hair: Seeking Power Through Resistance and Accommodation." *Gender & Society* 15, no. 5: 667–86.

West, Candace, and Don Zimmerman. 1987. "Doing Gender." *Gender & Society* 1: 125–51.

White, Deborah Gray. 1999. *Ar'n't I a Woman? Female Slaves in the Plantation South*. New York: W.W. Norton.

Williams, Christine. 2006. *Inside Toyland: Working, Shopping, and Social Inequality*. Berkeley: University of California Press.

Wilson, Midge, and Kathy Russell. 1996. *Divided Sisters: Bridging the Gap Between Black Women and White Women*. New York: Doubleday.

Wilson, William J. 1987. *The Truly Disadvantaged: The Inner City, the Underclass, and Public Policy*. Chicago: University of Chicago Press.

Woo, Deborah. 1995. "The Gap Between Striving and Achieving: The Case of Asian American Women." In *Race, Class, and Gender*, second edition, ed. Margaret Andersen and Patricia Hill Collins. Belmont, CA: Wadsworth Publishing, 218–26.

Zenner, Walter P. 1991. *Minorities in the Middle: A Cross Cultural Analysis*. New York: SUNY Press.

Zhou, Min, and John R. Logan. 1989. "Return on Human Capital in Ethnic Enclaves: New York City's Chinatown." *American Sociological Review* 54, no, 5: 809–20.

Index

About the Author

Adia Harvey Wingfield is assistant professor of sociology at Georgia State University. She earned her BA in English from Spelman college and her MA and PhD from Johns Hopkins University. Most of her research focuses on how intersections of race, gender, and class affect various minority groups' experiences in professional and nonprofessional workplaces. Harvey Wingfield's work has been published in several peer-reviewed journals, including *Gender & Society, Race, Gender, and Class, and Journal of Black Studies.*